William and Mary Commanda and the Algonquin Nation

William and Mary Commanda live near Maniwaki, Quebec, 83 miles north of Ottawa. They are members of the River Desert Algonquin Band.

William was chief of the band from 1951 to 1970. He worked for a number of years for a lumber company, travelling all over Quebec, through the United States and to the Maritime Provinces.

Mary is called Tanis by all those who know her well. She was given this name by her father who called her, naturally, *nind anis*—"my daughter" in Algonquin. She was born at Micomis, on the Gatineau River about 100 miles north of Maniwaki, while William was born on the reserve at the edge of town. Both in their mid-sixties at the time of

1. *William and Mary Commanda carrying a roll of spruce root from the woods.*

2. *Mary's father, Charlie Smith, sewing a birchbark basket.*
   Credit: Leonard Lee Rue III

the writing of this book, they continue to make the crafts that their people have made for millenia. Although Algonquin is their first language, they are both fluent in English and French, the two European languages of the area. In any normal day in their household, Algonquin, French and English are all spoken as a matter of course, depending upon the nationality of their visitors.

Mary's family had a log cabin on the Baskatong River north of Maniwaki. When they travelled from there, her mother would pack up all the gear in the morning—blankets, tents, food—and they'd start off. Mary's mother and father had the four children with them, the youngest usually in a *tikinâgan*, and they took along their hunting dog to complete the group. All the people and all the gear would go easily into their canoe, which was about 16 feet long.

THE INDIAN CRAFTS OF
WILLIAM & MARY COMMANDA

THE INDIAN CRAFTS
OF WILLIAM &
MARY COMMANDA

DAVID GIDMARK

STACKPOLE
BOOKS

Published in 1995 by
STACKPOLE BOOKS
5067 Ritter Road
Mechanicsburg, PA 17055

Printed in the United States of America

10 9 8 7 6 5 4 3 2 1

First paperback edition

Originally published by McGraw-Hill Ryerson Limited

Cover design by Mark Olszewski

Library of Congress Cataloging-in-Publication Data

Gidmark, David
    The Indian crafts of William and Mary Commanda / David Gidmark. —
1st paperback ed.
      p.   cm.
    Originally published: Toronto ; New York : McGraw-Hill Ryerson,
1980.
    Includes bibliographical references and index.
    ISBN 0-8117-2549-9
    1. Commanda, William. 2. Commanda, Mary. 3. Algonquian Indians-
-Industries. 4. Indian craft—Québec (Province)—Maniwaki.
I. Title.
E99.A35G48   1995
680' .89973—dc20
                                   94—16829
                                       CIP

Table of Contents

Preface

This book came to be written because of an acquaintance of several years that I have had with William and Mary Commanda of the River Desert Algonquin Band near Maniwaki, Quebec.

Known widely in Canada for their exhibitions of birchbark canoe making, the Commandas also continue to make a variety of Indian crafts, in addition to having many interests that touch upon Indian nationalism. Other Indians are known for specialties in crafts—the Huron for moose hair work, the Hopi and Navajo for turquoise jewellery, the Cree for beadwork and the Ottawa for quillwork—but few are as capable as the Commandas in such a wide range of Indian crafts. The Algonquin, Ojibwa, Abnaki, Chipewyan, Dogrib, Slave, Cree, Beothuk, Micmac, Malecite, Passamaquoddy, Penobscot and Têtes de Boule once made birchbark canoes. Today the Algonquin are the only surviving Indian makers of the birchbark canoe, and there are only four of them left.

I had an opportunity to serve an apprenticeship with the Commandas in canoe construction, snowshoe-making and many of their other crafts. Through many trips into the woods with them, I came to learn not only about their crafts but about Indian life and its close connection with the wilderness.

In December of 1978, William Commanda asked me if I would be interested in writing a book about the two of them and their crafts. The project was a natural for someone who had already published a book and was greatly taken by Algonquin culture.

It is not a common thing, understandably, for an Indian craftsman to take a white apprentice into his confidence. Naturally, William's suggestion that I write a book about them pleased me a great deal. We proceeded then over the course of nearly a year to gather material for the book.

This book could not have been accomplished without help in photography from Claire Poirier of Maniwaki, Quebec. Additional thanks for photos and photographic assistance is due to Michel Lemieux of Maniwaki, Leonard Lee Rue III of Blairstown, New Jersey, and Chris Kirby of the National Museums of Canada in Ottawa.

The Algonquin words in this book follow the orthography used in Lemoine's *Dictionnaire Français—Algonquin.*

As the reader will surmise from looking over this book, the chance I had to live among the last of the canoe-makers was much more than an interesting opportunity. It was an honour.

David Gidmark
Maniwaki, Quebec

She remembers her father putting out the fishing line from the canoe just before lunch and, as often as not, they soon had fish to eat. When they put in for the night they would first locate a good spot for the camp. Often Mary's father would get a deer in one of their camping spots. Then they'd stay there for two or three days to smoke the meat on a little smoking rack with a birchbark cover over it.

Mary's mother and father would paddle the canoe but her father always made little paddles for the children so that they could paddle along as much as they were able. "My father never jumped the rapids with us," Mary says, "we always portaged. My father and mother would only jump the rapids alone. My mother knew how to jump the rapids, although she couldn't swim. She would have sunk like a rock."

It was always Mary's father who would set up the tent for the night. The tent would have no floor but he cut out balsam boughs and piled them deep to serve as a floor. The blankets were then put on top of the boughs. Mary remembers how nice that was. "And I've been wanting to sleep on a balsam bed again for a long time," she says fondly. "You're so comfortable on it and it smells so good as you go to sleep."

3. *Charlie Smith in his eighties, working on a birchbark canoe.*
Credit: Leonard Lee Rue III

Her mother used to bring a smudge into the tent to rid it of mosquitoes. She smoked it up for a while and opened it just before they were ready to go in for the night. Mary says that it did a good job in keeping the bugs out.

Mary tells many stories about her parents, whose first language, of course, was Algonquin. A retiring woman anyway, her mother became even more diffident when she had to express herself in English or French. When she built up enough steam to get angry with someone, she nevertheless tempered her anger with a certain politeness. "Go to hell, please!" she would say.

Her father, Charlie, called *Kickanakwat* (Broken Cloud) in Algonquin, travelled all over western Quebec as a guide for the missionaries. Long journeys by canoe used to take him to Parent, Trois-Rivières, Waswanipi, Timiscaming, and other places far afield.

It was intended that Charlie become a medicine man. To do that he would have had to go to the top of Manitowadjing, the highest hill for miles around the Maniwaki area. A young boy nine years old was required to make a fast, alone, for nine days. He could only be nourished by maple syrup brought from time to time by a designated older person. Young Charlie was afraid to go on the hill by himself for so long, so he missed his opportunity.

William is at his feisty best when the subject of Indians comes up. Whites and Indians from the Maniwaki area were called to a special meeting in town some time ago to discuss provincial game policy and regulations. The province sent its minister in charge of such things to the meeting.

When the time came to announce the policy towards the Indians, the minister very benevolently told of all the concessions in terms of game regulations that the province had planned to accord to the Indians.

William stood up in front of the entire assembly and told the minister for the province of Quebec not to pat himself on the back. The privileges he was awarding, William told him, were not the province's to give.

Pierre Trudeau visited Maniwaki while he was prime minister and William was chief. According to William (the story may be apocryphal; it's hard to tell with him sometimes), the prime minister was anxious to find out his views on the situation of the Indian throughout Canada. Was there anything specific he didn't like?

William thought a moment. "I don't like something about your court houses," he said. "You've got a word spelled wrong. Justice."

"I believe it's spelled the right way," Trudeau said.

"No," William suggested. "You should have spelled it J-U-S-T U-S."

For many years, William worked for a large lumber company. The company of course deducted withholding tax on his income. However, William believes that to claim a refund on his taxes would be to recognize the validity of the white government, something he refuses to do. So for more than twenty years, he has been adamantly against claiming a tax refund, something that could have netted him several thousand dollars a year. In addition, William prides himself on never having taken any welfare money. Nor does he believe that Indians should resort to violence to take back the country that they lost.

In 1968, a number of Indians from the Canadian side of the border between the United States and Canada were having difficulties in passing customs. Freedom of passage had been guaranteed by the Jay Treaty.

Many of the Indians who went back and forth had been those who worked on high towers. It was work that was important to them, work for which it was difficult to find other workers. Two demonstrations were organized in 1968 to protest these difficulties and the business was finally taken care of. Micmacs, Malecites, Algonquin and Mohawks had grouped together to stage the protest. William was among them.

This is not the first time William and Mary or their family have figured in a book. William and Mary are both mentioned in a book entitled *Artisanat Québécois*, about crafts within the province of Quebec. Likewise, they have figured in a few books by Bernard Assiniwi.

Mary's father was pictured making a birchbark canoe in a book published in the United States several years ago.

William's father, Alonzo, was a well-known man in the woods around Maniwaki. In 1944, John Durant wrote an article about Alonzo Commanda for the *Saturday Evening Post.*

Durant had fished with Alonzo for years, coming up from the United States nearly every fall for a canoe trip mixed with fishing. His article is highly laudatory. In fact, its title is "The Best Guide in the World." But, as he explains, every fisherman thinks his Indian guide is the best. So his article is more or less a tribute to all the "best guides."

Nevertheless, he has some remarkable feats of Alonzo's to report. At the annual fair in Trois-Rivières there was a contest to see who could carry a 200-pound sack of sand the longest distance. Alonzo, carrying the sack around a track for 8 miles, was the winner. He weighed slightly over 150 pounds.

Another story about him has it that, after shooting a bear from his canoe, he had to go back into the woods about a quarter of a mile to retrieve it. Tying a tumpline to the bear, he carried the 500-pound behemoth back to the canoe.

4. *The last of the old canoe-makers. Charlie Smith, Mary's father, at the age of 81, with David Makakons, 80, at Rapid Lake in western Quebec.*
Credit: Leonard Lee Rue III

He was a likeable man, according to Durant. Maps meant little to him on canoe trips, his judgment often being better than the maps.

At that time, Alonzo was trapping 50 miles north of Maniwaki. He would go up to the trapline in October and not return until the ice went in May. Taking a pair of huskies, clothing, and a lean-to tent, he would also bring some provisions that supplemented the moose he always shot on arriving in his trapping territory.

The meat of the moose gave him enough to eat for the whole winter and the moose's hide furnished him with *babiche* (rawhide strings) for his snowshoes. He also netted some trout and was able to shoot a partridge when he needed one.

The Commanda household in Maniwaki is also home for Mary's brother, Basil, now nearly seventy. He worked most of his life as a guide for a hunting and fishing camp at Desert Lake. He continues to trap in the fall and still acts as a guide for an occasional hunting or fishing trip. In the traditional Indian way, Basil is a very quiet and shy man. When visitors come to the house William never fails to introduce him: *"Il est mon beau-frère. Il n'est pas beau, mais il est mon beau-frère pareil."*

William and Mary worked at the same hunting and fishing camp, William joining Basil as a guide. They say today that those were their happiest years. They enjoyed the tourists they worked for, although there were nevertheless a few problems from time to time; some of their oddest stories concern the occasional uncooperative tourist.

One of these was a tourist who was extremely cheap. He and his Indian guide took off in the bush to fish for a few days. This man was not particularly easy to work for and when they returned, the Indian guide left. The tourist came into the kitchen of the lodge where Mary was working, shaking his head, very perplexed. "I can't understand why that guide quit me," said the tourist. "I did everything for him. Everything. I even gave him a cigar."

Another time there was a particularly cantankerous tourist who left for a day's fishing with one of the guides. He had a list of complaints and verbal abuse to offer the poor guide. "Paddle this way. Come back a little. How come we aren't getting any fish? Why are the mosquitoes so bad?" After such a stream of babble, the guide quit when he arrived back at the camp. Another man was assigned to the irritating tourist and the same thing happened; the guide jumped the job. The problem repeated itself with the third guide.

The situation by now called for some special attention by those in charge. The manager of the camp thought finally that he had just the man for the job. Romeo Smith, brother of Mary and Basil, was given the impossible tourist. Romeo went off happily with him for many days and came back without a complaint—Romeo had been born with a hearing impairment.

Around the Commanda household, one of the standards applied to certain endeavours is whether or not Indians would do it in that particular fashion. A short while ago, William and Mary began to build a cabin in the woods at Lemay Lake, 50 miles north of Maniwaki. This occasioned a summer of hustle and bustle, during which many worked on the project and almost all lent their advice. As the cabin was being finished, William and some helpers put up a good solid outhouse to serve the cabin. Basil surveyed the outhouse, shook his head in disapproval and said, "But that's not the Indian way."

William keeps abreast of current affairs and offers opinions on subjects as wide-ranging as the Middle East, rising food prices, the white régimes in South Africa and even the men's magazines, "Playboy and Pentax" (as William refers to them).

The jogging fervour that had recently developed did not fail to attract William's attention—not as a participant but as an observer. However, he had a different term for the sport. *Pajog* is the Algonquin slang word for penis. To William, the occasional runner who passed by was going *pajogging*, which, loosely (and decorously) translated, could be taken to mean woman-chasing.

There are, or have been, perhaps thirty tribes which belong to the Algonkian family—but a few bands in western Quebec and eastern Ontario are the only ones that bear the name Algonquin (occasionally spelled Algonkin).

Algonquin culture, reflected here in the crafts, is different from other North American Indian cultures. The crafts are different, beliefs are different and even the languages are quite dissimilar from one another.

The Algonquin followed the game for food. For this reason, it is probable that in prehistoric times their settlements were short-lived and their chiefs undoubtedly did not exercise the power that chiefs of other tribes did.

They were a people highly respectful of nature; prayers and offerings were frequently given when taking something from the woods.

Algonquin, trappers and hunters who ranged all over the Ottawa River Valley, had gathered in numbers at the mission in Oka, Quebec, near Montreal. There was a settlement there for at least 200 years.

Iroquois had also settled at Oka. The two villages apparently lived in peace, if not harmony, until the mid-nineteenth century. Rivalries developed and a large part of the Algonquin population, lead by *Pakinawatik* (Tree Struck by Lightning), second chief at Oka, moved to the confluence of the Gatineau and Desert rivers where a reserve had been set aside by the government. *Pakinawatik* was William Commanda's great-grandfather.

In 1913, Frank Speck, the American ethnologist, spent some time with the Timiskaming band of the Algonquin and also with the Timagami Ojibwa band. The Timiskaming band is the next Algonquin band west of the River Desert Band in Maniwaki. Although known as Ojibwa, the Timagami band is the band immediately west of Timiskaming.

These two bands, and Speck's paper on them, are particularly interesting because they give an insight into groups similar to the River Desert Band, and at an early period.

The basic social unit was the family, which was composed of individuals related by blood, along with women who married into the family. There was a family name but individuals had nicknames taken from an animal, a personal characteristic or a deed.

An important fixture in the life of these bands was the hunting ground. Each family had one, where the male members of the family had exclusive rights to hunting and fishing. Should anyone else trespass upon the hunting ground, he met with great disapproval. At the very least the transgressor was the object of conjuring from a shaman in the offended family.

Hunting for pleasure was probably unknown among the Indians. Families often allowed others to hunt in their territories, particularly in times of scarcity. In such cases, a family might obtain the right to hunt and fish along a certain river or stream until their fortunes took a turn for the better. If a family found it necessary to kill game on another's territory, the pelts were delivered to the owner later.

These Indians kept very close account of the game on their hunting grounds to avoid depletion of the stocks. This went as far as taking a census of each beaver cabin. Often they had a self-imposed restriction on hunting a certain species for a year or longer.

Towards the end of summer, the Algonquin gathered to set off to their hunting territory. All their hunting equipment and fish nets were prepared in advance.

Small game was plentiful; the moose was in the rut and had to be killed soon so that its meat could be dried for the coming winter. Women dried the meat, and also berries for the winter's coming.

The families then made a birchbark (or sometimes hide) wigwam or tepee in a favourable spot where they could confront the cold months. These tepees were highly practical. If there was a slight space under the bark at ground level, a draft was created which sent smoke from the fire out the apex of the cone. Light and detachable, they were often transported and reinstalled elsewhere. The tepee was so portable because it was made out of smaller sheets of birchbark which could be easily undone *(5)*.

5. *Birchbark tepee.*

Hunting season was followed closely by trapping season, and trapping was a skill for which the Algonquin, in particular, were renowned. The meat of most of the trapped animals was eaten; furs were used as clothing, or, with the coming of the white man, in trade.

It is axiomatic that the Indian made extensive use of the animal he killed. A moose furnished raw material of all kinds. There were the food uses—the great mass of meat that modern hunters use (hopefully), but also the delicacies—the tongue, the nose, the brain, genitals, heart and liver *(6)*.

6. *Mary roasting a moose nose.*

Other parts of the moose had what might be called craft-related uses. The skin was used for clothes, but also for blankets, as a covering for shelter, and as tumplines and snowshoe harnesses.

Rawhide was used to lace snowshoes. Moose hair was used in embroidery, now very rare. Intestines and sinews could be used in sewing. Leg bones became knives or scrapers for hide; shoulder bones were used as shovels. Other bones were used as sewing needles, arrowheads or fishing hooks, or for decorative inlays in paddles. Teeth were used in jewellery. Horns became weapons and knife handles.

Last but not least, excrement was sometimes used for fires on wet days.

The old people decided who would marry whom, and the woman married into the husband's family. Marriage had to take place outside the clan. The children then became part of the husband's family.

In the Timagami band, according to Speck, the birth of a child was the occasion for a feast to which all the relatives were invited. When the child was a year old it was given a name. This was time for another feast. The food was passed around the assembly, and so was the child—for everyone to kiss.

The child then kept this name for life, unless a funny or outstanding incident occurred later which would cause him to be given a nickname.

When Mary's youngest brother Charlie was born, her mother said to a neighbour that a bat had come that same morning. And the neighbour said that Charlie was going to be a night bird, out every night. And when Charlie grew up, he stayed around the house all day and only went out at night.

It was Cecilia Gagnon who delivered young Charlie and most of the other children. They were delivered at home and she always boiled Indian medicine to ease the labour.

The *okima* (chief) was the head of the group. The chief had to look after the welfare of the widows and orphans of the tribe. He would also do some counselling. If punishment of a band member were called for, the chief would call a meeting at which proper chastisement would be decided.

The *okima* always had two auxiliary chiefs. If the chief was ill, or away hunting, the second chief took over. The third chief was responsible for collecting provisions for feasts. And if meat came into the camp, it was his job to apportion it.

In the Timagami band the dead were buried in the trees. Bodies were wrapped in birchbark (which the Algonquin also did, William says) and then placed high in the branches of the spruce tree. The burial spot was chosen for its beauty, at a place along the river where the dead person could watch his relatives passing by.

The Indian hunters had many taboos in regard to the game they killed. Individual hunters would always eat a certain part of the animal first. These taboos grew out of personal experiences, such as a dream warning the hunter not to eat another part of the animal.

The bear was a highly respected animal. His skull was painted and tied to a spruce tree shorn of bark. The hunters placed the antlers of moose and caribou on tree stumps. Others would see this and would know that the hunter had shown proper respect to the animal. To forget to do this was to shirk one's duty as a hunter.

The Algonquin of Maniwaki and western Quebec had an extensive mythology.

Windigo was a human who ate human flesh and then became a spirit. Mary's father said that even a bird that ate bird flesh became a *windigo*. It was then called *windigo pinecinjic* (*windigo* bird).

Pakwadjininiwak (bush men) were little harmless men that would tease the sugar-makers in the spring.

Misabe was a big spirit, a giant, who lived in the woods. He had big footprints, like Sasquatch.

Memingwesiwak were spirits that dwelt under the rapids. They were smaller than Indians and had flat noses.

Pagak was a spirit that people would sometimes hear when they travelled at night. Only his bones could be heard. If a person allowed himself to be frightened by it, he soon died. Anyone who was not frightened by it was not harmed.

Wiskedjak was a playful spirit. He played tricks on the people but was most often on the losing end of his own jokes.

The material culture of the Indian, like many of the culture's other aspects, is dying quickly. Pressures are brought to bear upon the Indian craftsman. Most of these pressures stem from the Indian's need to work for wages. His crafts suffer—or are extinguished.

Another related problem is that the buyer of the craft wants as good a deal as possible. A good buy means inexpensively priced—not a piece of art, not quality. The best Indian craft, if sold at a price that reflected the minimum wage for the labour involved, would be far beyond what most people would be willing to pay.

The craftsman has two choices: price his crafts unfairly low (to him), or make souvenirs, which are quick to produce, for the tourist trade. If he opts for the latter, the survival of quality traditional craft is imperiled.

That is not to say that modern tools cannot be used. Sewing, formerly done with fibers or with nerves of various animals, is now done with commercial thread. Steel knives and needles have long since replaced those of bone.

Around Maniwaki, some of the crafts that have apparently been forgotten are the making of blankets and clothes of rabbit skin. *Wabozekwai,* Mary calls the blankets. She can barely remember having seen one. Her mother used to make them. They were loosely woven, so much so that she could see through them. But they were warm blankets and were used mostly for babies.

Baskets of ash-splint, another lost art, are rarely made today, although they were quite common years ago.

It may be only with the birchbark canoe that the Indian craftsman gains what would be considered elsewhere reasonable remuneration for his work. That remuneration still does not equal the pay of, say, a postal worker or a bus driver in a city—who pays less for his commodities where he lives.

A great part of the Woodland Indians' life was their medicine. Almost all had some knowledge of medicine, but there were members of the tribe who had special knowledge of medicinal herbs, and they were always sought out by the others. The Ojibwa had their medicine society, the *Midewiwin,* with all its attendant ritual. The Algonquin, though knowing most of the same medicinal herbs, don't seem to have had such an established organization relating to the use of medicine.

Mary has an especially good knowledge of Indian medicine. We once made a trip into the woods to look for birchbark for a canoe. William and I went off with the saw to cut down a tree that he had spotted earlier; Mary stayed with the truck. It was nearly four hours later that we returned. The average person would have been bored by such a wait, but Mary had wandered in and out of the woods along the road, looking for medicine. She was happy to have found three or four types of medicine to take back with her. The woods were her home and she knew what to look for there. It was as if she were shopping in a pharmacy.

The list of Indian medicines is seemingly endless. The older the medicine person, usually, the more he or she remembers of the medicine, indicating that this knowledge also is disappearing fast.

Kapisibunkweiak is an herb that must be taken frequently. Its purpose is to alleviate weakness.

Ozawadjíbik (yellow root) is good for liver ailments, particularly hepatitis.

Muckikobak is the plant we call Labrador tea, among other names. It was a frequently-used tea of the Algonquin. It has a 2-inch leathery-surfaced leaf that has a velvety underside and is steeped in boiling water to make the tea. The tea is soothing, good to drink before going to bed. A very similar plant, *wisakibak*, with a shiny surface on both sides of the leaf, is poisonous, so knowing the difference between the two is important.

Wikenj, another extremely popular herb, is used for coughs, colds, and cramps. We call this plant calamus. A little of the root is shredded and put into a cup of boiling water. It is ready to be taken after it steeps and is cool enough to drink.

For fever and piles, among other things, Mary uses *cikakwack*.

Another root, *tipwebanodjîpik* (pepperroot), is put in the mouth and chewed and the juice swallowed to stave off a cough.

According to Mary, a very effective laxative is balsam gum. You get the gum in little hard drops directly from the tree and swallow a little.

As already mentioned, certain people were particularly good at Indian medicine and gained a reputation for their skills. They were paid for their medicine. If they weren't paid for it, the medicine would not work.

Mary says that when an individual went to get medicine in the woods, he had to leave an offering, as she herself still does. Today, whenever she fetches *muckikobak, wikenj* or any of the others, she leaves some tobacco. If she happens to be short of tobacco, she leaves a penny, still upholding the tradition that an offering must be made for whatever is taken from the woods.

Much of the medicine was gathered in the fall of the year, before the leaves fell, but some could be harvested all year long. Dried, it could be kept indefinitely.

White medicine is based, in large part, upon Indian medicine. There were many white people in the town of Maniwaki in the old days who used to come to get medicine from the Indians. Doctor Mulligan, one of the old doctors in town, used to tell some of his Indian patients to go home and take their own medicine when they came to see him. He made much of his own medicine but he saw the curative properties of much of the native medicine. Of the several doctors in town, he was the lone one who had much faith in Indian medicine.

Although in this book the Commandas are able to share some of the crafts practised by their ancestors, one thing they would have a hard time sharing is the Algonquin language.

It has been estimated that the Indians of North America spoke over two hundred languages. Most of these were as different as, say, English and Russian, or French and Chinese.

Many Indian languages were related, however, and were said to be in the same language family. Thus Algonquin is in the Algonkian linguistic family, the widest-ranging Indian language family geographically, extending from the Micmac and Naskapi in the east, to the Cree in the north and the Blackfoot, Arapaho and Cheyenne in the west.

In practical terms, though, the only tribe with which the Algonquin could easily communicate would be the Ojibwa.

If it is true that any culture is best reflected in its language, it is unfortunate that the Indian languages are so inaccessible to non-natives. The Algonquin language, for one, is a splendorous thing. To begin to study the Algonquin language is to realize immediately the stupidity of the portrayals on television, which have the Indians uttering little more than "ugh." The white student of the Algonquin language would take a long time before he progressed beyond the Indian equivalent of "ugh."

Algonquin is a systematic, highly complex language. Although its vocabulary is not as extensive as that of English, its grammar is more sophisticated. The growth of the Algonquin vocabulary compares to that of the English language.

In Algonquin there are thirteen cases of nouns. Verbs can be conjugated in nine modes and seven tenses. The verb *kiwe* (go back) has 355 conjugations (according to this writer's count). The same verb in Spanish would have just over eighty and in French it would have about 100 conjugations. The verb for "put" (there are no infinitives in Algonquin, strictly speaking) would have again the same number of conjugations in Spanish and French respectively, but in Algonquin, because the verb is transitive and is modified according to the nature of the object(s) being described, its form *(aton)* would have 1238 conjugations (again according to this writer's labourious count).

In Algonquin, verbs are the key parts of speech. There are more verbs in the language than any other part of speech. To indicate the colour red, for example, one does not add the adjective for red. Instead, it is necessary to conjugate the verb that means *be* red.

To say "I see him," one says *ni wabama*, with the pronoun and the verb in the usual order and the verb itself conveying the fact that there is a direct object. However, to say "he sees me," the verb ending is changed, becoming *ni wabamik,* and the subject and object in the phrase are reversed without changing the original order of the words.

These few cold grammatical facts are given to suggest that we should have more respect for the Indian languages. In the recent past in Maniwaki, as in too many other places, Indian children were punished for speaking their language in school. Government teachers taught the English language, thinking little of Algonquin, or of French for that matter, which is the most predominant European language in the area. The Algonquin language is now dying out, and there are few who realize what is being lost.

It is in the poetry of their references that the Indian languages have become famous. Everything in the language was tied to the culture and the natural environment. Witness the Algonquin names for the months of the year:

January	*kenôzitc kîzis*	"the long month"
February	*akâkodjic kîzis*	"ground hog month"
March	*nïka kîzis*	"wild goose month"
April	*kawasikototc kîzis*	"month when the ice goes"
May	*wâbikon kîzis*	"month of the flowers"
June	*otehimin kîzis*	"month of the strawberry"
July	*miskwîmin kîzis*	"month of the raspberry"
August	*otatakâkomin kîzis*	"month of the blackberry"
September	*kakakone kîzis*	"harvest month"
October	*namêkos kîzis*	"month of the trout"
November	*atikamek kîzis*	"month of the whitefish"
December	*pitci pipon kîzis*	"month of winter's coming"

The Algonquin word for winter, *pipon,* was also used for year. To them, two years ago was two winters ago. They had names for the seasons we know—*sîkwang* (spring), *nibin* (summer), *takwakik* (autumn) and *pipon* (winter)—and one of their own, *anicinabe nibin* (Indian summer), when the last of the leaves had fallen from the trees and the days were warm.

Other words expressed concepts or problems with which we aren't familiar. The verb *wabanic* meant "surviving until spring." To name a rainbow, they used the word *takwanipihisan.* It's literal meaning is "coat that the rain wears."

For someone with a taste for the wilderness and linguistics both, an Indian language is ideally suited. The Indian vocabulary is centred on the natural habitat. The languages have adapted somewhat to present needs, though, with some interesting results. In Algonquin, the United States is referred to as *Boctonenang* (land of the Bostonians). People from New England were the first whites to contact the Algonquin, from the area which later became the United States.

Learning an Indian language gives an insight into the culture of the people who lived in harmony with nature. Respect for the environment is manifested through their language.

Added to the complex linguistic heritage of the Algonquin is the vast store of knowledge about plants in the woods. Ethnobotanists have catalogued over 500 different plants that have been used by the Algonkians for food, medicines and for technological purposes. Some plants have uses that fall into many different categories. The study of the botany of the Algonquin is, like each facet of the culture, a fascinating undertaking in itself.

Tanning of Moose and Deer Hides

Moose Hide Tanning

Of all the work involved in making Indian crafts, perhaps none requires as much elbow grease as the tanning of moose hide *(mônzwaian)*.

The hides of large animals were important to the Algonquin. They were used mostly for clothes, but also found use as blankets, tumplines, and material for making decorative craft.

In the Maniwaki area moose is the most common large animal, although the northern limit of deer nearly reaches the town and a number of these hides are available. Hunters often bring deer and moose hides by the Commandas' house during hunting season.

According to William, when his father was a boy caribou *(ininätik)* also ranged in the area. His father told him of once crawling over ice on a reserve lake with his grandfather to sneak up on two caribou. They were not common even at that time; those are about the only two that people in the Maniwaki area talk about.

William and Mary and their families never killed a moose without putting the hide to good use. When William was young he used to go to a hill with other children and bring a moose hide to slide on. They slid on the hair side, causing the hair to fall off and leaving the hide nearly tanned.

Instead of feathers, Mary's mother used to put dry moose hair *(mônz opiweian)* into a pillow tick and make a pillow from it. Moose-hair mattresses used to be made in much the same way. The mattress was shaken every day and then turned over, and it lasted many years.

When out camping in the bush, they'd sometimes put a moose hide under them and a blanket on top. "But don't ever roll yourself in a fresh moose hide when it is cold," William says, "you'll never get out of there; it will freeze solid."

In the old days when Indians killed a moose, they almost never took the moose hide in quarters. They would bury the moose in the snow and leave it there for a few days. It would be hard to skin but the delay would have a tenderizing effect on the meat. According to William, "Small animals might sometimes dig down to the meat, but the wolf will stay away from it because he doesn't like to eat meat he hasn't killed himself."

A moose hide should be tanned when it is fresh from the kill, as it is much easier to scrape at this time. If Mary has to preserve a hide before tanning it, she covers the meat side with coarse salt and rolls the raw hide up, meat side in; prior to working with it, she must soak it for several days to make the hide supple again and to get all the traces of salt out. But it is preferable, and easier, to work on the hide while it is still fresh.

Mary used to do a lot more tanning of moose hides than she does now. It is heavy work and really for a young person, although in the past it was generally considered women's work.

Moose hides vary in thickness for a number of reasons. A small young moose has a thinner hide than a large old moose. "The moose hide starts getting thicker from June to December," Mary says, "after December it starts to get thin again. We like to get moose hide in the spring when it's easier to tan. Deer hide gets thicker in the fall too, but in the spring it's thin as paper. So we look for deer hide in the fall."

The first step in the tanning process is to remove the hair from the hide. It is at this point that the hair is saved and used for pillows and mattresses, if desired. If Mary wants to do this she washes the hair thoroughly and then dries it.

The hide is draped over a stick or otherwise aligned so that the long knife blade has a flat surface across which to cut. The knife blade is sharp and because the hair is hard on the blade, it must be sharpened often *(7)*.

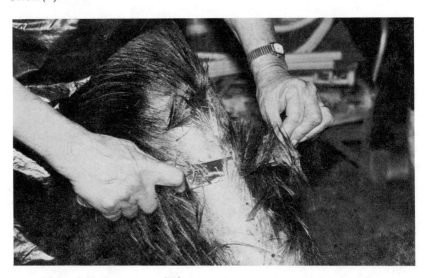

7. *Cutting hair from moose hide.*

Then it is time to scrape the hide. If the hide has been left to dry, Mary soaks it in water for a day or so to make it possible to scrape it. If she has a hide that has been around for a long time, she sometimes adds lime to the soaking solution, since this seems to help in making the hair roots come off more easily. A full moose hide is heavy. From my own experience, I would say that a full-sized wet moose hide with hair on weighs upwards of 100 pounds.

Mary then puts the hide on a scraping log *(tcicakwahiganatik)*, hair side up. A scraping log is a hardwood log that has been split in half and fixed up on one end with two legs. It usually comes to just below belt level, where substantial pressure can be applied. The bark is taken off the log so that it provides a smooth scraping surface.

Mary puts a plastic garbage bag on a cord for use as an impermeable apron. The wet hide also stinks, and the little apron keeps the clothes protected. The hide is held to the scraping log as Mary leans against it.

With the hair side up, the hide is scraped with a dull knife. A little bit of scraping is done carefully and then the hide is repositioned. By working her way over the hide, always scraping away from herself, Mary eventually finishes all of the hide *(8)*.

8. Scraping moose hide.

If the hunter has done a poor job in skinning, as often happens, knife marks show up later on the meat side of the hide. These marks extend deeper than the scraper scrapes, so that they remain there. If the hide is smoked on one side only—always on the hair side—then this is not so important. If both sides are to be smoked, then the moose should be very carefully skinned. Rather than a hasty job with a hunting knife, the skinner could take more time and perhaps use a beaver-skinning knife.

Long ago, the Indians used the shank of the moose for a scraper. As mentioned, the fresher the moose hide, the easier it is to scrape, but it is never easy. That is why today it is very rare to find smoke-tanned moose hide. Factory-tanned moose and deer hides are about the only ones used today to make moccasins and other crafts.

It takes much pressure to scrape the hair and sinew from a hide, but all the same, Mary is careful not to exert too much pressure. If she were to do so, she could put a hole in the hide, ruining it for any large projects. It would still be all right for moccasins and other small items, though.

After the hide is completely scraped on the hair side, it is turned over to the meat side. Care is taken to completely rid both sides of hair and fat and sinew. Otherwise, the hide does not tan well, nor does it smoke properly. However, if the hide is only being scraped for *babiche,* care is not as important.

A stretching frame *(cîngabidjigan)* is then made to stretch the hide. This frame consists of four hardwood poles tied at the corners to prevent the hide from pulling it toward the centre. The stretching frame can be set either horizontally a foot or two off the ground, or at an angle. Either position is designed to make it easier to work the hide. Mary has to be careful to estimate the size of the frame properly, since the hide will stretch as it is being worked. Whenever the hide loosens sufficiently, the ropes around the perimeter are again tightened. The frame is always somewhat larger than the diameter of the hide.

9. Cutting slits on perimeter of hide.

While the hide is still in the soaking pan, Mary pinches the edges and makes a hole with a knife. *(9).* Placed every 5 or 6 inches, these holes make it possible for the hide to be bound to the frame.

Mary then wrings the hide out well *(10* and *11).* This is done by

10. Working moose hide with hands.

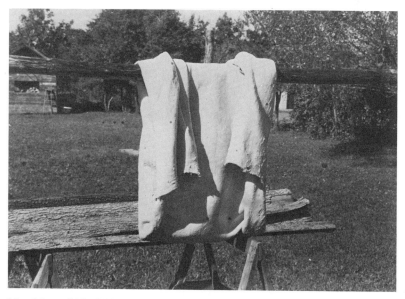

11. Moose hide folded for wringing.

twisting the water out between two hardwood sticks *(12)*. When the hide is as well wrung-out as possible, less time is required to work the moisture out of it on the stretching rack.

12. Wringing out moose hide.

13. Moose hide on stretching frame.

At the top of the frame, Mary begins in the middle of the rope, lacing the hide to the frame in one direction, then returning to the other half of the rope to lace the hide around in the other direction *(13)*.

Mary's tool as she works the hide is a small hoe that has a dull steel edge. The hide is hit repeatedly, so a sharp-edged knife would cut it. The hide is then beaten until dry *(14)*. The beating causes the hide to stretch little by little. As it stretches, the lacing on the side is tightened. In this way, the hide is stretched to a larger surface area.

14. Hitting hide on stretching frame.

This beating of the hide until dry takes a few hours, depending on the moisture in the air and the moisture that was left in the hide when it was wrung out. The frame is often set up in a shady area if there is direct sunlight, so that the hide does not dry too fast.

When it is dry the hide is sprinkled with grease, using a little spruce branch *(15)*. Mary sometimes uses commercial cooking oil, sometimes animal grease for the job. The dry, oiled hide is then taken from the frame and soaked in soapy water overnight and the whole process of stretching, beating, drying, and oiling is repeated the next day. Even when the hide is soaking in the softening bath, it is worked vigorously with the hands to help soften it.

15. Sprinkling moose hide with grease.

16. A tcicakosidjigan.

As the hide dries on the frame, sinews on the meat side are picked off until it is as clear as possible. Often at this stage, raw spots still remain in the hide. These are worked with particular care, both by beating and when soaking in the softening bath. Much labour is also expended on a rubbing board, called a *tcicakosidjigan (16)*. This is a dull-pointed board fixed to a base. The hide is pulled hard from both sides over the point of the board. The rubbing board is a great boon for working hides, allowing Mary to concentrate her strength in one area of the hide *(17)*.

17. Working hide by hand over tcicakosidjigan.

When Mary has softened the hide so that it becomes white and soft as a blanket (always the result of many *days* of work), it is ready for smoking. Mary always waits for a clear, dry day to do her smoking, since the smoking does not take as well on humid days. While occasionally a hide is used white, most hides are smoked, chiefly to add colour. The smoking may also aid in preserving the hide, which may not be entirely tanned. It is the fine tawny colour and the smoky aroma of the hide that are so attractive to connoisseurs of true Indian craft.

Properly tanned skin does not have any holes in it. Should there be any, though, Mary sews it up to keep the smoke from passing through it. She may also simply close any holes temporarily with a piece of wood.

Mary often has to wait for ideal smoking conditions. To avoid dampness and wind, she also likes to do the smoking indoors. Recently she has been able to do this in a shed, but before that she often did it in the kitchen of her old house. While the conditions there were favourable, the air naturally was thick with smoke.

The hide is placed over a tripod and covered with canvas or some other cloth that will keep the smoke in. A smudge is then made below the hide *(18)*.

18. Preparing smoking pot.

Mary gathers punk wood *(pikidjisak)* according to the type of hue she wishes to have on the hide. Spruce and poplar, among others, give light hues; cedar and yellow birch give a deepened tan. The usual time for smoking is about twenty minutes. A longer period of smoking, however, gives a deeper colour *(19)*.

In making her smudge, Mary is careful to make only smoke and not fire, as a flame would only burn and harden the hide. If she smokes the hide only on one side, it is the hair side that is smoked. The inside (meat side) remains unsmoked and would go on the inside of the moccasins or whatever item she is going to make.

Tanning of hides in days long passed was the work of women. But it is a very arduous work, which explains why smoke tanning has become a rarity today. Smoke-tanned moose hide is fast becoming a very expensive commodity. Costing more than three times as much as factory-tanned hide, smoke-tanned moose hide—when it is available—sells for more than $7.00 a square foot.

19. Mary smoking hide.

Mary Commanda is virtually the last woman in the Maniwaki area to continue the smoke tanning of hides, and probably one of the last in Canada. Most Indian craft today is made with factory-tanned moose and deer hide. Mary continues to make as much of her craft as she can with smoke-tanned hides.

Mary's son once took orders for moccasins from some of his friends at the Department of Indian Affairs in Ottawa where he worked. She made several pair of smoke-tanned hide.

After her son had delivered the moccasins, his friends started hanging the moccasins outside to get rid of the smell. And they asked the boy to ask his mother if there wasn't something they could put on the moccasins so that the smell would go away. This was more than a little ironic, not only because these requests were coming from the Department of Indian Affairs, but also because people who appreciate true Indian craft look first of all for the evocative aroma of smoke-tanned hide.

Deer Hide Tanning

Mary considers the tanning of a deer hide a blessing next to the amount of work it takes to tan a moose hide. A deer hide (*wawackêciwaian*) is light to begin with. And it doesn't have to be beaten as a rule. When working a deer hide with the hands, there is not such an amount of brute force required.

Otherwise, the tanning process is very similar to moose hide tanning (p. 27), with only a few alterations.

Deer hair, for instance, is not as hard to get off as moose hair so that if the hide is fresh, the scraper can take the hair off.

A deer hide is wrung out in a different manner than a moose hide. After scraping, the hide is wrapped around a stationary pole and a heavy stick which is then twisted with both arms. The tree and heavy stick should both be clean or dirt may stay on the hide.

The hide is hung from a pole about 6 feet off the ground. Mary works it by hand until dry. She pulls it in all directions to loosen the cellular fibers of the dermis and help it to dry all the way through. This does not have to be done continually but does have to be done regularly so that the hide does not dry stiff. After Mary works it for a while with her hands, she turns to the rubbing board. The dull point of the board works into the hide as the hide is passed back and forth over it.

It's very easy to get deer hide dirty during the tanning process. The dirt does not come out but stays in the hide and shows up even after the hide is smoked. Mary takes pains not to dirty the hide by making sure that the rubbing board is sitting on a clean surface. Also, in wringing out the hide, she makes sure that both of the poles she uses are very clean. Hidden dirt in the poles comes out quickly under the pressure being exerted to wring out the hide.

An alternative way of working the hide is the method Mary uses for moose hide—cutting holes around the perimeter of the deer hide and lashing it to a square frame of hardwood poles set off the ground. She does this infrequently with deer hide, however, as the deer hide is much thinner than moose hide and the simpler method is just as effective.

The process of working the hide manually can take a day, although it need not be continuous work. Mary sets up her hide in the morning and works it a few times an hour during the day, taking time out from her other household chores. There aren't too many trilingual women in this country who can put an apple pie in the oven and then go downstairs and work on a moose hide or deer hide.

A variation in the tanning of a deer hide is tanning the hide so that the hair stays on. Travelling in the woods, Mary's father often took such a hide with him and used it as a sheet when he made up his bed for the night. This kind of hide makes a very good insulator, but nowadays is most often used for rugs. Because of its tendency to shed, it is rarely seen as decoration on apparel.

Mary first takes a fresh deer hide and scrapes it on the meat side only. If the deer hide is a little old, she would first have soaked it for a day or so in water, at the same time washing off the salt used to preserve it.

The hide is put on a rack of the same sort that is used to stretch the moose hide, although the rack for the deer hide would be proportionately smaller. It is stretched meat side up.

Then Mary liberally salts the meat side. The salting of the meat side fixes the hair on the reverse side.

She leaves the hide stretched and salted on the rack until it is almost dry. Then she scrapes away the salt and the hide is left nearly white on the meat side. It is oiled (common cooking oil works well) until the skin is penetrated and then washed again. As it dries it is pounded with a dull-bladed hoe or similar instrument until it is dry and supple. If it does not appear sufficiently tanned after the first go-through, it is again oiled, washed in water and pounded thoroughly.

Once again the hide is washed so that it will be clean and all the soap will be out of it. Then it is worked with the hands to make it more supple *(20)*. Sometimes Mary must work for hours to get it to the right stage.

20. Working deer hide with hair on.

If the hair will be left on to serve as a rug, it is not necessary to tan the hide completely. In fact, a partially tanned hide with some stiffness will always lie flat on the floor. A hide that is completely tanned will bunch up like a thin cloth rug *(21)*.

21. *Deer hide rug.*

Snowshoe Making

Snowshoes *(âkimak)* were used in Asia, in crude form, thousands of years ago, but they only became the sophisticated implements we know today at the hands of the North American Indians, particularly the Woodland Indians.

Eskimos, as a rule, did not use snowshoes because their travel was mostly over ice and hard-packed snow. The Woodland Indians developed the snowshoe which provided the only means of conveyance during the winter through very deep snows of the forest. It is believed that the Algonquin, specifically, developed the lacing pattern that is used today on most snowshoes. However, the actual form of the snowshoe varies from tribe to tribe, within a tribe and even from buyer to buyer, because years ago the Indian craftsman often made the snowshoe to the specifications of the person who ordered it.

William says that his father only made the snowshoe frames. "He never really learned how to lace; that's funny, isn't it? He used to scrape hides but others always did the lacing for him."

"They took their snowshoes with them in the fall and left them there over the winter. They hung them in bushy spruce branches and when they went back the following fall, the lacing was black because of the rain. The sun didn't get to them though; they were always left in the shade. Sometimes a squirrel would chew on the *babiche,* so there were always repairs. A lacing job would last one year. It had to be redone every fall. A lot of people knew how to fix them but not too many knew how to lace them. White trappers in town always had their snowshoes laced by the Indians."

William and Mary ordinarily make snowshoes for sale every fall and winter. William gets the wood from the bush and prepares the frames; Mary cuts the hide and does the lacing.

The size of the snowshoe depends on the size of the person to be using it. The heavier the person, the longer and wider the snowshoe. But any individual should try to use the smallest snowshoe that will support him well. It is important that the snowshoe not be too heavy for the wearer. Dragging an extra pound along with the feet is equivalent to carrying several extra pounds on the back. Also, the size of the snowshoe is sometimes varied according to the condition of the snow.

To make the standard snowshoe, called by the Algonquin *sîkwang âkim (22)* or "spring snowshoe," William cuts a straight log of white ash, *âkimâk* (the name comes from its use), which is 8 feet long and without a knot. The white ash used for the snowshoe should have approximately thirteen or fourteen annual rings to the inch. In the east, the ash has that many annual rings to the inch in the northern United States and southern Canada. North of this, ash grows slowly and the wood is too brittle. Farther south than this, it grows too fast and is susceptible to easy breakage.

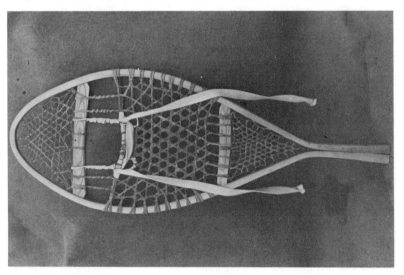

22. Sîkwang âkim.

In the same manner that he prepares the gunwale of the canoe from a cedar log, William splits the ash log in quarters, splits away the heartwood and splits the remaining piece lengthwise again until it is down to the approximate size he needs.

Then he takes the 8-foot stick and carves it down on the carving horse (like a carpenter's saw horse) until it is uniform, 1 inch thick and ¾ of an inch wide, with the annual rings visible on the width.

He shaves this 8-foot stick in three spots—for a short length where the major bend forming the toe will be, and the two spots where the stick will join together to form the tail.

The stick is steamed in boiling water for ten minutes and then bent around a snowshoe form, tied and left to dry for a day or two (*23* and *24*). As it is removed from the form, two dummy cross-pieces are fitted across the frame during drying.

23. Bending snowshoes.

24. Tying snowshoe tail.

After the frame is dry, the real cross-pieces are fitted into the frame. The front part of the snowshoe is called the toe, the middle part the foot and the part just in front of the tail is called the heel.

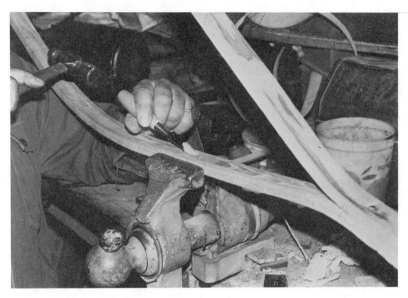

25. Cutting snowshoe cross-bar mortise.

Carved also from white ash, the two cross-pieces *(okwikin)* are mortised into the frame and are carved in crescent shape to allow a little more room for the lacing of the foot *(25)*. The edges are slightly sanded to make for round edges so that the snowshoes will not scrape each other in use. The frame finished, it awaits only the lacing.

In today's commercially made snowshoes, the rawhide most often used is cow. The Algonquin used deer, moose, caribou and a number of other hides. The Commandas continue to use moose hide almost exclusively in their lacing.

After the moose has been skinned—hopefully as deftly as possible to lessen the work later—the hair is cut off with a sharp knife. Work with hides having been traditionally women's work, Mary does the cutting of the hair and then proceeds to scrape the hide on a scraping log. She scrapes the hair on both sides, hair side and meat side. With a dull knife (instead of what she used in earlier days—the sharpened leg bone of a moose) Mary works very hard to scrape off the remaining hair on the hair side along with a superficial layer of skin. Scraping for rawhide is not as meticulous a job as for tanning, when sloppiness will be apparent on the tanned hide. A convenient difference between making *babiche* from a hide and tanning the hide is that *babiche* can be made from a smaller piece, a moose quarter for example, while Mary most often likes to have a hide remain whole for tanning.

Once the hide is scraped on the hair side, it is turned over and scraped on the meat side. And, after perhaps eight or ten hours of extremely hard work, the scraping job is done.

Cutting the hide into long strips is another laborious task. An entire moose hide can take a full week to cut into rawhide. One moose hide may furnish enough rawhide to lace ten pairs of snowshoes. Special attention is paid to sections of the hide that lend themselves to the right places on the snowshoe.

The foot of the snowshoe has to support the foot of the wearer—significant weight, in other words. For this section, heavy, thick rawhide is cut from the part of the hide where it is thickest—at the neck and on the middle of the back. If the hide is too thick to cut conveniently, it can be stretched on a rack, frozen and then thinned with a knife at these locations.

Lacing for the toe and heel, which do not have to support much weight and hence can be laced finely, is taken from the legs and belly—thinner areas of the hide.

For the cutting of the hide, the portion to be cut is placed over half of a small block of wood sitting on a table. The hide is then rotated, so that five or six strands can be cut at the same time. William built a cutting table that helps with this chore and shortens the cutting time significantly.

The skin is pulled against a knife fixed in the table. A small, spring-held brace just ahead of the knife holds the hide snug against the table so that it meets the knife properly. The hide is rotated on the table and cut so that a very long strip of rawhide results *(26)*.

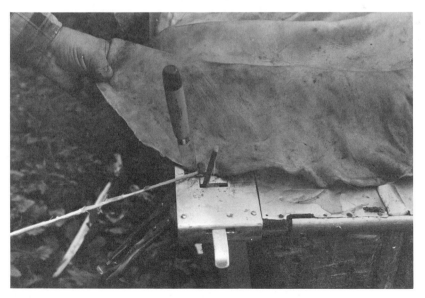

26. Cutting babiche.

Once the hide is cut into lengths, it can be dried until used. Before lacing however, the hide must be wet. It is laced snugly onto the snowshoe frame and dries very tight in a matter of hours. If the lacing were not tight, it would slow the speed of the person walking with the snowshoes.

It is interesting to note that, while shapes of snowshoes varied widely among tribes, lacing patterns always adhered to certain principles.

The lacing could not be too supple. It was always bisymmetrical. Each "stitch" was supported by another. There was always valid reason for every over or under, around or through. So, although there were different shapes and sizes, there was no such thing as a bad lacing pattern.

There is no easy way to describe how to lace a snowshoe. It might be said that lacing snowshoes, somewhat unlike other procedures, is not taught so much as it is learned. About the only general statement that

27. *Mary lacing snowshoes.*

can be made is that lacing procedures done first on the right side are then repeated on the left. It is very difficult to learn how to lace a snowshoe; the beginning lacer might gain some idea after a bare minimum of one week of constant, all-day attempts. One of the best ways to learn lacing is to follow, step-by-step, the lacing pattern of a snowshoe that has already been laced *(27)*.

A beginner at snowshoe lacing might practice on a frame with ordinary grocery string. There is a difference, of course, between this and *babiche*—*babiche* tightens as it dries—but it is easy to get an idea of the pattern with string. And there is no wasted *babiche*.

It takes over 50 feet of *babiche* to lace the foot of a snowshoe. And, although the pattern is nearly always the same, the mesh can vary according to the thickness of the rawhide, and the type of rawhide used.

In the standard snowshoe that the Commandas make, the mesh is such that the lacing comes to the side of the frame ten times. Decades ago, when the last of the *nowaia âkimak (28)*, or soft snow snowshoes, were being made, the beaver rawhide mesh used in them was so fine that the lacing came to the side of the frame forty times. The rawhide was pencil-tip thin and necessarily much longer.

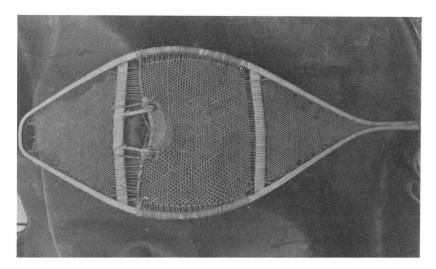

28. Nowaia âkim.

The snowshoe harness is a length of tanned hide that is made fast to the top reinforced piece of rawhide. Its purpose is to hold the toe secure so that it can move neither forward nor back nor laterally. However, it allows the heel to move up and down freely so that the tail of the snowshoe stays on the ground as much as possible. Thus, the natural movements in walking lift the toe of the snowshoe up for the next step.

It was especially in the *nowaia âkimak* that woods other than the common ash were used for the frames. Among other woods used were yellow birch, black cherry, and white birch.

To the Algonquin trapper, his pair of snowshoes was indispensable. In fact, his life often depended upon them. So all trappers of long ago were familiar with the construction and repair of snowshoes, and, as with the birchbark canoe, the particular workmanship of one crafts-man could often be recognized by another.

Baskets and Spoons

The birch tree lends itself to many uses. It is the bark of this tree, perhaps the most versatile of all, that is especially used for so many purposes. One of the most common uses of the paper birch was in making the birchbark basket *(wikwemot) (29)*.

29. Decorative birchbark basket.

Mary's mother put maple sugar in birchbark baskets. They were also used as water containers, for they were normally water-tight. If they were not, a small amount of spruce gum was added at any cracks. Instead of putting her household leftovers in pans, Mary's mother would put them in birchbark baskets, then place the baskets in a swamp to keep their contents cold. She also used to put blueberries in a birchbark basket, berries that she had cooked until they were almost dry; they finished drying in the basket and would thereafter keep indefinitely. When the family was travelling, they could just cut a piece of the dried blueberries, put sugar in it (some of the sweetness had been lost in drying) and eat it.

Another of the many uses for birch bark was as covering for shelter. Mary's grandmother, who was born around the year 1850, often constructed wigwams of birch bark out on their trapline or in the spring sugarbush. They would usually return to these year after year.

Charlie Smith, Mary's father, learned how to make a birchbark wigwam from his mother. He made several of these. Charlie's wife did not like his pipe, so whenever the family moved to a new location, he built a new birchbark wigwam in back of their cabin. Charlie would then have his daily pipe alone in the wigwam.

Charlie built a birchbark wigwam in 1952 that is still standing. It is about 140 miles north of Maniwaki, and is 17 feet high and about 17 feet in diameter at the base. As many as seven people can sleep in it. The fireplace is at the centre of the wigwam. When the draft is properly adjusted, the smoke passes out through the opening in the top. The birchbark sides of the wigwam do a good job of keeping the heat from the fire so that it is comfortable inside even in low temperatures. In summer, the draft can be adjusted so that some smoke remains within the wigwam to keep out the flies.

For her baskets, much the same as when she searches out bark to make a canoe, Mary tries to locate birch bark that is blemish-free. However, because the baskets are small, it is not so crucial that the tree be nearly perfect. The range of quality is much wider than for use in canoes.

Bark should never be taken from a birch tree just for the fun of it, or only to build a fire. Mary takes bark from a birch tree only when she has good use for it. The custom of her people dictates that she leave an offering for anything harvested from the woods. William and Mary are saddened today when they see a campsite where birch trees have been defaced only to start campfires.

Birch trees are not as commonly felled to get bark for baskets or other small objects as they are to get canoe bark. The most sought after bark, as with canoe bark, is the winter bark that can be peeled off from the tree in winter (with the aid of boiling water) or in late spring or early fall. In winter bark, the dark inner cambium comes off with the outer bark. Not only is this bark stronger than summer bark, but its dark layer allows for designs to be made on the bark.

A good time to get winter bark is during Indian summer, after a few frosts have come and when a warm day or two occurs. Bark peeled on a hot day, say over 80°F, almost falls off by itself. If the weather is cooler than this, it often takes great care to get the bark from the tree without tearing it.

When the bark is taken from the woods, it is rolled inside out and tied. It is ordinarily then laid flat and pressed to stay flat until it is used. Bark fresh from the tree can be used immediately; if the bark is not used within a few days, it may have to be soaked for some time before it is pliable enough to work with.

The lacing material of the birchbark basket is most often the root of the spruce tree. These roots, dug out of the ground a few feet from the trunk of the tree, are not strong singly but when they are stitched to make a seam or when they are wound several times around a gunwale, they have surprising strength. Added to their strength in combination is the fact that they shrink somewhat as they dry, tightening the bond significantly. The Indians at Rapid Lake, north of Maniwaki, travel often with their cars along bush roads. It is not unknown for them to repair a fallen muffler by tying it up with *watap* (spruce root). One strand is easy to break; together they make a formidable binding.

Mary splits the roots in half according to the method described in the section on the making of the birchbark canoe (p. 109). Then the roots are rolled into small coils and boiled. Fifteen minutes of boiling is usually sufficient to loosen the bark of the root, which then comes off easily. Too often if the root is not boiled, the bark adheres to the root. In this case, it is only by laborious picking that the bark will come off.

When the bark is off, small branches left on the root must also be removed. Mary can then separate the roots by their diameter so as to be able to do even stitching on the basket. The stitching is a long job, the more so on highly elaborate baskets.

Prepared roots can be kept as long as desired. They dry out—and become brittle in drying—but Mary has only to soak them for a while to restore them to suppleness.

Perhaps the easiest of the birchbark baskets to make is the basket that the Woodland Indians used to collect maple syrup. The four corners of a birchbark sheet are folded in so that there are no seams in the finished basket. These are held in place with two small split sticks. For a more permanent basket, the side can be stitched. This is an excellent emergency basket in the woods if no other container is available *(30)*. It can actually be used to boil water: the basket is half filled with water and as long as the flame touches the bark at an area

30. Berry-picking with temporary birchbark basket.

that has water on the other side of it (i.e., not above water line or at folded corners) the bark will not burn. (It is ironic that one of the best materials in the woods for building a fire on dry or wet days can also be used to make a container to boil water.)

The typical Algonquin basket is a cube-shaped one that may be almost a miniature, or may be as big as 2 feet on a side, depending on the needs of the maker. Mary makes a miniature basket that she fixes on a piece of leather. The basket can then be worn around the neck. The larger sort of basket is durable, generally lasting longer than the temporary kind made for collecting maple syrup or for emergency use. It may also be ornately worked with spruce root decoration or designs on the bark, if it has been made with winter bark.

A standard pattern is used for the cube-shaped basket *(31)*. The bark is cut to the size desired, then folded, white side inside the basket, so that the side pieces overlap slightly *(32)*. If Mary finds it at all difficult to fold the bark, she has only to soak it for a while until it again becomes supple.

After the basket is folded, Mary uses an awl to make the holes along the seam. The holes, made through the bark at regular intervals, are first held with pegs that Mary shapes quickly from a stick at hand. She sharpens the point of the stick and breaks off the temporary peg in the hole *(33)*. This allows her to form her basket well before sewing with the spruce root. The sewing, as she removes the pegs one by one, is less awkward for her than it would be without them *(34)*.

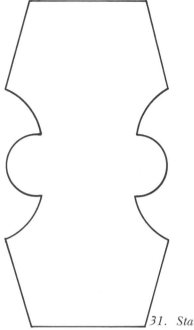

31. *Standard pattern for birchbark basket.*

32. *Folding bark for basket.*

33. Pegging side of basket.

34. Sewing side of basket.

35. Sewing rim of basket.

Once the basket is formed, Mary sews a rim on it *(35)*. This rim is either a small green branch wound around the basket at the top or it may be a thin piece of ash that has been soaked for a short time. To fix the rim on the basket, she makes holes below the rim with the small awl and then sews with the spruce root, putting the root twice through each hole continuously around the rim on top *(36)*.

36. Mary working on birchbark baskets.

To make a lid for the basket, Mary cuts out a piece of bark slightly larger than the outer perimeter of the rim. She then cuts another strip of bark, slightly stiff and about ½ inch wide, that will be sewn perpendicular to the first piece as the sleeve of the lid, so that it fits snugly against the inner side of the rim. The top part of the lid is doubled by sewing another piece to it. This not only reinforces the lid but hides the stitches on the sleeve.

Curved Spoon

A very useful spoon *(mitikomïkwân)* can be made from the lower trunk of a small hardwood tree. Not as difficult to make, perhaps, as a burl spoon (p. 58), it can be of almost any size and is just as useful.

First, a tree is located that is growing in a cluster of two or three. The crowding causes the lower part of the trunk to curve. William chops out the part of the trunk that he is going to use, the bottom section.

Because the piece can split along the grain, he can split from either the middle or the top. The first split gives the rough form of the spoon *(37)*.

Rough forming of the arm and cup of the spoon is done with an axe

37. Splitting for spoon.

38. Shaping spoon with axe.

(38). Care must be taken here, as the fingers could suffer considerably in any mishap. William's missing thumb is not a result of spoon-making, but it could have been.

The initial hollowing of the cup of the spoon is done with a chisel, continued with the crooked knife and polished off with sandpaper if desired *(39).* In use it takes on its own finish.

39. Hollowing out spoon with chisel.

Burl Spoon

In prehistoric times, the making of a burl spoon or bowl was truly a lengthy chore.

The burl was split from the tree with a wedge made from a deer antler, then abraded to rough shape with a flint instrument. The bowl was burned with hot coals and then scraped with flint. This process was repeated until the bowl was deep enough. The bowl was polished by grinding with sandstone, first coarse and then fine.

William still makes burl spoons from time to time but his methods are somewhat more modern. Felling a maple (maples seem to have more burls, and they make for a tough spoon), he chops off excess wood quickly with an axe before taking the piece home to do the fine work *(40)*.

40. Roughing out a burl spoon.

He soaks the piece of wood in water so that it won't dry too quickly and crack. Using the crooked knife, he carves the handle down to the proper size. The versatile round tip of the crooked knife allows him to fashion the bowl of the spoon.

When the spoon has been properly roughed out, he gives it a smooth finish with sand paper. If he wants to bend the handle, he soaks it for a few days, bends it and then fixes it to dry.

Although he does not put any preservative or varnish on the completed spoon, it takes on a nice dark finish after some use *(41)*.

41. Finished spoons.

Beads, Quills and Moose Hair

Beadwork

Mary says that when she does beadwork *(masinikwasa)*, she has the feeling that what she is doing is not really Indian craft. She believes that quillwork was the true Indian decoration. But beadwork has been adopted so widely that quillwork—especially that which is of high quality—is extremely rare.

It is thought that the original beads were made of stone, shells, grains, and bone. All of these had to be painstakingly worked to be utilized. It is no wonder then that glass beads were the first of the white man's materials adapted by the Indian to his craft. Beads were an item of trading soon after the first contact, finding their way into typically Indian motifs. Floral Woodland patterns that had been made with quills could now be made with beads. The typically Woodland designs were also used on baskets and occasionally on canoes *(42)*.

42. Floral Woodland patterns.

Prehistoric beads were made of almost anything animal, vegetable or mineral. Mineral beads included those made of copper, hematite, quartz, serpentine, magnetite, slate, soapstone, turquoise, encrinite sections and even pottery. Nuts and seeds also found their way into beadwork. From animals, artisans took shell, bone, horn, tooth, claw and ivory to make beads. Later work made use of silver, porcelain, and glass.

Beads were used in many ways. They were tied in the hair, worn from the ears, on the neck, arms, wrist, waist and legs. They decorated bark and wooden bowls and matting and basketry.

Wampum was a kind of bead used frequently in trade. It was usually made out of clam shells. Their usual colours were white and purple, or a combination of the two. Ordinarily thought of as woman's work, their manufacture was very difficult. No account of the original process of making wampum exists. The process of manufacture was first noted in the mid-seventeenth century, probably somewhat evolved.

A piece of clam shell was removed with a sharp hammer. It was then put in a cut in a stick and ground to an octagonal figure about an inch in length and half an inch in diameter. The piece was then fixed to a bench. A drill was made from the untempered blade of a handsaw, ground into the required shape and tempered in a candle flame. This drill was then placed in the top of the small cylinder and rotated rapidly with a bow. A small vessel was placed over the drilling operation. Drops of water fell from it continuously to cool the drill so the shell wouldn't break. When the drill was half-way through the small cylinder it was reversed, and drilling began from the opposite direction.

For finishing the surfaces of the wampum bead, a wire about a foot long was fastened at one end to a bench. Directly under this wire was placed a grindstone, run by a foot treadle. There was a groove in this grindstone into which the beaded wire was worked. The beads on the wire were turned with a small flat stick in the other hand, all the while being worked in the groove of the grindstone. In this way the wampum beads got a smooth, lustrous finish. They were then put on strings about a foot in length.

Wampum had been a means of exchange among the Indians. When the whites came to the continent, they began using wampum as a medium of exchange with the Indians, and even among themselves.

William has wampum belts that are several hundred years old. He regards these as sacred and therefore takes them out only for ceremonial occasions or to show a friend. They are not pictured here because William considers them religious objects.

The most common beads in use today are the small spherical beads that are called seed beads. These are the beads that Mary uses most often. They have a hole in the centre and are usually of a clear glass. The variation in available colours is almost limitless. Vials of beads, with up to 500 beads in a vial, can sometimes be purchased for as little as $0.25.

Needles for beadwork with seed beads are commonly longer and thinner than ordinary sewing needles. They are also more difficult to thread. In fact, all beadwork is invariably hard on the eyes. Size 16 beading needles can be purchased for around $0.20 for a pack of six. The needles are so thin that they are easy to bend while working with them, particularly when the work involves stitching through hide.

The easiest type of beading is done on a loom. Mary can make bands of beads for belts, headbands or for other types of designs that require rectangular work *(43)*.

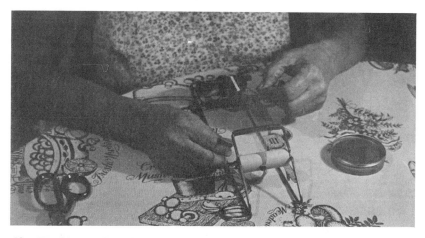

43. Working on bead loom.

The loom stretches the warp threads tight. If eight rows of beads are to be made, nine warp threads are used. The threads are stretched and put into little grooves in the loom and both ends are wound around a screw on a wooden roller. The roller on each end of the loom can be loosened and tightened so that a long piece can be woven if desired. The weaving is rolled up on one of the rollers as it is completed. To have a piece of greater length, the strings must be longer. For a piece of greater width, Mary simply adds more warp threads.

The technique Mary uses for weaving on a loom is called the *double-weft* method. After first working out the beading pattern on a piece of graph paper, the beads are strung on the needle in the proper colour sequence. The needle is passed completely under the warp threads. The beads are slid off the needle, down the thread and pushed up under the warp threads, one bead in each column. Mary then holds them there with the index finger of her left hand. She passes the needle with the right hand back through the beads on top of the warp threads. At the end warp thread, the needle is loaded again with the proper colour sequence of beads and turned around to pass back under the warp threads once more. Possible decorations with loom work are generally limited to rectangular designs or ones with diagonal lines.

The appliqué stitch is more difficult and harder on the eyes. Mary draws the design she wishes to make on the hide she is working with. Her needle comes through the bottom (meat side) of the hide first. Three beads are threaded onto the needle and, with the beads sitting on the hair side of the hide, the needle is passed back through the hide. If the beads have a tendency to spread a little to much, she passes the thread through the three beads again, making a circle with the thread. If the beads have lain flat against the pattern, she can continue stringing three beads at a time to finish the design. Beadwork done in this manner is extremely painstaking and people who are familiar with Indian craft realize that prices for good beadwork, whatever they may be, are probably cheap.

Quillwork

It is said that in the Woodlands, quillwork was a common decoration until the middle of the nineteenth century. Then beadwork and certain types of embroidery became more common.

It would probably not be an exaggeration to say that women capable of doing quillwork are as rare as the makers of the birchbark canoe. It is difficult today to find quill-decorated boxes for sale. When they are available, they are usually expensive. In view of the work it takes to decorate birch bark with quills, a substantial price is not difficult to understand.

One of the few places in Canada where quillwork is still done is on Manitoulin Island in Georgian Bay, Ontario. The work there is of fine quality. In Maniwaki, because the craft is infrequently done, it has a tendency to be less developed. This work is still done in a handful of places, but it is likely to disappear even sooner than other remaining skills. In a day of increasing hourly wages, work with quills is not really a paying proposition.

When doing work with porcupine quills, Mary tries to find a dead porcupine on the road. "If we killed a porcupine for a little bit of quills, we'd be wasting a porcupine," she says.

44. Sorting quills by size.

She pulls the quills with her bare hands but she has to be careful as the ends of the quills are barbed and very prickly. Before she uses them, she culls the short ones from the long *(44)*. Those of the same length are used together.

Mary soaks them in water for a short time before using them; soaking makes them supple and less likely to break.

In order to make a design on bark, she first traces two parallel lines about an inch apart. The width of the lines establishes the length of the "stitch" made by the quill.

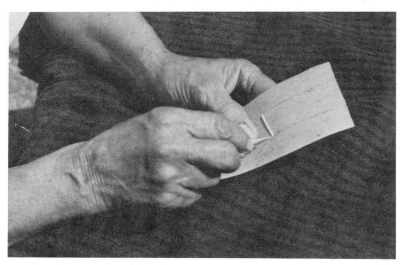

45. Putting porcupine quills in bark.

She then uses a fine-tipped awl to make a hole in each line. An end of the quill is put through each hole; later they will be folded back *(45)*. Mary uses her fingers to pull the quill through the hole, but in case of difficulty, tweezers would be employed *(46)*.

The next two holes are put alongside the first two, so that when the next quill is stitched in place, it is parallel to, and rests snug up against, the first quill. The pattern is continued until the desired grouping of quills is complete.

Following these principles, Indian women created small baskets entirely covered with quills. Generally these quills were dyed. Their coloured and intricate patterns are today quite rare.

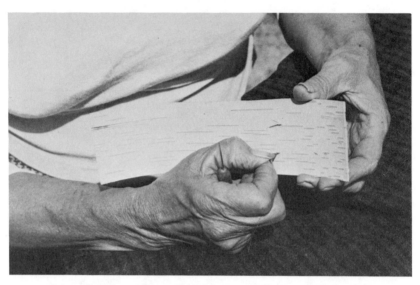

46. *Pulling quills from under side.*

Moose Hair

Moose hair work is another disappearing craft in North America, one largely supplanted by other types of embroidery and by beadwork. It is still done in such places as Loretteville, Quebec, and at a few other reserves in the east. It compares to quillwork, not only in its rarity, but also in technique.

Use of the hair for decoration illustrates again the Indians' ingenuity in making use of nearly all parts of the moose's carcass. Moose hair is cut from the hide in one of the first steps of the tanning process.

Then it is washed and dyed any one of a number of colours. Traditionally natural dyes were used for the dying process; today Mary uses commercial dyes almost exclusively. She finds it easier to use the darker colours, as the lighter ones don't always take.

Moose hair decoration is put on almost any hide product. It is most commonly found on moccasins, but it can also be done on shirts, bags, and so on. Hair for this type of work comes from the mane and jowls of the moose, although hair from elsewhere on the hide may be used for certain work.

Years ago very intricate embroidery was done with moose hair. In some of this work, each hair was put on one at a time.

The hair is separated according to length and colour, if some of it has been dyed. A small bunch of hair is cut and fastened to the hide *(47)*. This is done by sewing a bundle to the hide with a loop of the thread and then tying the thread *(48)*. Then Mary turns the hairs up and forms a miniature bouquet with it *(49)*.

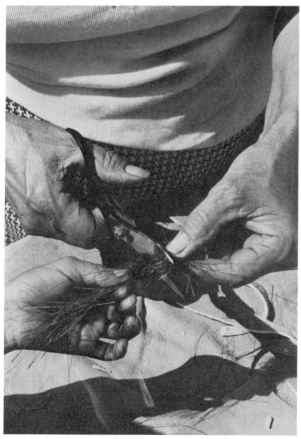

47. *Cutting moose hair.*

48. *Sewing moose hair to moccasin tongue.*

Other possibilities for decoration usually involve fixing the moose hair to the hide with thread so that different designs are formed. The old technique of true embroidery is almost never seen.

49. *Moccasin patterns with moose hair work.*

Apparel

Moccasins

The word "moccasin" comes from the Algonquin (or at least Algonkian) word for shoe. *Mäkïsin,* as the early philologists wrote it, has virtually the same pronunciation as moccasin.

Mary makes snowshoe moccasins of moose hide for heavy winter use, and other moccasins of deer hide for lighter wear. The lumberjacks in Maniwaki used to buy their snowshoe moccasins from the Indians. Mary's mother often sold them. She could sometimes make as many as twenty-two pairs of the slipper-size moccasins from a large moose hide.

William also made much use of the moccasins in the old days. "We had snowshoe moccasins for the snowshoes. We never knew about rubbers in those days. Before I started working in forestry, rubbers were unknown to me. I had never used them before. Then I began to find that they were no good for your legs; they caused rheumatism. You got sweaty and you could freeze your feet. Rubbers are never good because no air passes through. Smoke-tanned moccasins allow your feet to breathe through them."

"We'd use snowshoe moccasins just for the dry season. Coming on spring we'd have what we called oil tans. We got them at the shoemaker's. Before the coming of the white man, the Indians made their own from moose shanks."

Mary frequently used sinew *(atis)* from the back of the moose for sewing—for moccasins, hats, tumplines and other items—but for the past thirty years or so, she has been using commercial thread. "When we were in the bush and we had no thread, we had to use it," Mary says, "if we had moose around." They called it Indian thread.

Mary cuts the first pieces she will use for the moccasins from a pattern traced on the hide *(50 and 51).* She decorates the tongue of the moccasin in a number of different ways. Always done before the sewing begins, this decoration might be beadwork, moose hair decoration, thread embroidery or other forms. All the sewing is done inside out, the better to hide the stitching of the seams. She begins the sew-

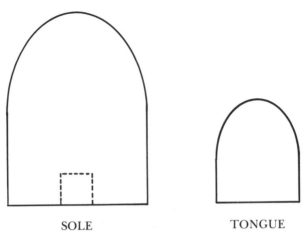

SOLE   TONGUE

50. Pattern for moccasins.

51. The two pieces of the moccasin pattern.

ing at the toe of the hide, joining the tongue and sole cut-outs. This requires careful stitching as the puckering around the toe must be even *(52)*. One of the ways of telling good moccasins from poorly made ones is the evenness of this stitching. It is said that the Ojibwa got their name from the word in their language for this type of puckered stitching. (Another explanation has it that the word comes from the Algonquin roots *odji* [meaning slurp, more or less] and *abwe* [bouillon], because of the way the Ojibwa customarily drank their soup.)

52. *Mary sewing puckering on moccasin.*

When the toe is sewn, Mary folds the back of the moccasin sole and cuts out a little square. Folded back once again and sewn in an inverted T, the heel of the moccasin is formed.

If the moccasin is to have a lining, Mary sews it along the original pattern, inserts it into the moccasin and sews it to the hide at the ankle.

To make a snowshoe moccasin, Mary begins as though with a normal low moccasin. However, the hide, usually moose, is thicker. And if it is smoke-tanned hide, the wearer will take care not to wear it in wet snow, as it stiffens readily and the stiffness has to be worked out laboriously by hand.

A snowshoe moccasin does not usually have a liner; the wearer instead may have two pairs of wool socks.

The main difference between snowshoe moccasins and other moccasins is that snowshoe moccasins have an ankle piece that is sewn to the top of the moccasin (53). This added piece helps keep the ankle warm and the snow out. The ends of the piece are crossed in front of the ankle and tied with leather straps across the front and around the ankle.

SNOWSHOE MOCCASINS

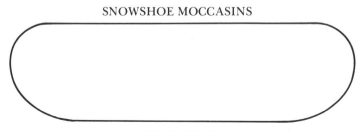

ANKLE PIECE

53. *Pattern for ankle piece on snowshoe moccasins.*

Mittens

Not long ago, a man who happened to be a provincial game warden came by the Commandas' house while they were in the middle of their work day. He stood around and watched and chatted for a while and then mentioned that he went deer hunting every year in Pennsylvania. He made the following offer: "I'll bring you a raw hide some time; and all I'll ask is a pair of mittens."

Perhaps the man thought he was doing the Commandas a service. The greater likelihood is that he just didn't think at all. The work in tanning the hide and making the mittens far outweighed any value the raw hide might have.

That said, it is necessary to add that mittens are one of the easier things to make in terms of Indian garments. Mary ordinarily uses deer hide, most often smoke-tanned, for the mittens she makes. If she intends to make linings for them, she smokes the hide only on the hair side. The mittens, like other items made with smoke-tanned hide, can get stiff if they are wet. But then, they are intended for use in cold, dry weather.

Mary first measures the customer's hand for the width of the pattern. She then cuts the hide for the top and bottom of the palm. A piece of hide is cut for the thumb from another small pattern. And, if there is going to be a gauntlet on the mitten, this is cut from another pattern *(54)*.

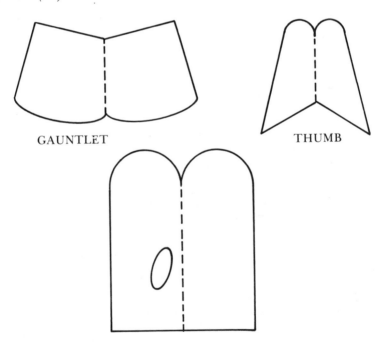

GAUNTLET   THUMB

54. Pattern for hide mittens.

The pieces of the mitten are all sewn together with the mitten inside out, so that the stitches will not be seen when the mitten is reversed. A welt is used in all the seams for strength.

Mary makes a lining of either flannelette or wool for all her mittens. Made from a slightly smaller pattern than the hide mittens, the liner is sewn to the mitten around the edge of the wrist.

Although making mittens is one of the less difficult of the hide crafts to make, a beginner would do well to proceed slowly so as not to do an uneven job on the mitten. It took Mary years of working at it to make it look easy.

Beaver Hat

When Mary makes beaver hats, she sometimes uses beaver that she has trapped herself. There are a number of trappers in the Maniwaki area, however, who bring her their own beaver pelts to have made into hats. When she tans the beaver, she does not tan it completely, as a little stiffness in the hide helps the finished hat to hold its shape.

She first measures the customer's head with a tape measure. Then she cuts two pieces of the beaver hide of equal size. These are then sewn together inside out (55). The thread she uses is a very strong combination of polyester and cotton, heavy on the polyester. Mary no longer uses sinew for this job, although that was what she used years ago.

55. *Sewing beaver hat.*

After the two pieces of pelt are sewn together, she sews in a silk lining and turns the hat back right side out (56).

56. William and a beaver hat.

Jacket

In a conversation with a friend recently, the subject of Grey Owl came up. Grey Owl was an Englishman who lived as an Indian in Canada in the first third of this century. He eventually authored four books on the wilderness. To say that he had a colourful personality is understating the fact.

My friend remarked that Grey Owl was given to exaggeration—as he certainly was. However, one thing my friend was using as a gauge was the fact that Grey Owl was wearing hide clothes in the period from 1910 to 1935 "when the Indians didn't even wear them any more."

Did they? I wasn't too sure myself. I assumed, as my friend had, that Grey Owl's wearing of hide clothes was another of his affectations. Until I saw in a book on Grey Owl a photo of an Algonquin friend of his, Dave White Stone, who wore hide pants. So I asked William and Mary and they told me it was not uncommon to see Indian trappers in the Maniwaki area wearing hide pants well into the 1940s and later. Frank Meness of the Maniwaki band wore hide pants almost up until he died in the early 1970s. He never wore the pants inside the house and didn't wear them at all for the last few years, but earlier he had worn them frequently.

Speaking to a man who had been a factor for the Hudson's Bay

Company at Rapid Lake, the Algonquin settlement 90 miles north of Maniwaki, I learned that he had seen people wearing hide pants in the 1940s and 1950s with regularity.

Hide pants are less common than hide jackets. The Commandas know no one who wears hide pants today, except on ceremonial occasions. In terms of large items of apparel, only hide jackets continue to be worn. Tourists buy these regularly and they provide income for several women in the Maniwaki area who still make them.

Mary has made many hide coats *(kapotawaian)*. She made one for Pierre Trudeau on the occasion of his visit to Maniwaki. She believes that he still wears it from time to time.

In order to make a full man's jacket, Mary needs more than a full moose hide, perhaps a hide and a half or even two hides, if they are small. Or she may use the equivalent in deer hides. She must get many pieces from the hide—the front and the back of the jacket, as well as the sleeves, collar, pockets, lapels, and fringes. These last, sometimes not included in a jacket, take up more material than one would imagine, although they can be made with spare pieces.

Mary first cuts all the pieces she needs, doing most of the cutting from patterns (57). In almost all of the seams of the jacket, Mary sews a welt, which is an extra piece of hide sewn between the two main pieces. This welt helps make the seam more secure and more even as the stitching is done inside out and the stitch remains inside of the finished jacket.

57. Pattern for moose hide jacket.

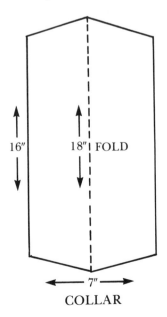

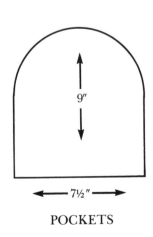

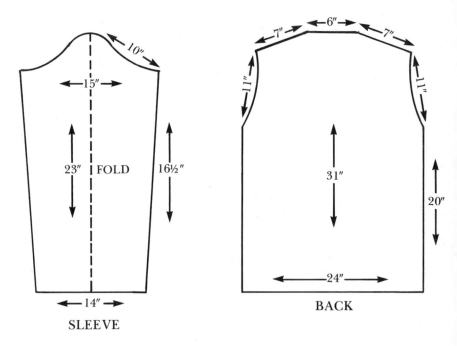

SLEEVE

BACK

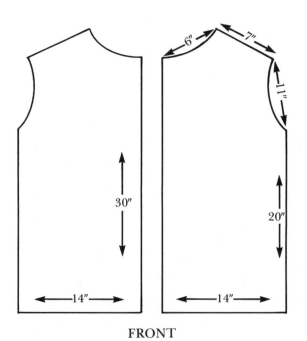

FRONT

Needless to say, if the seam is stitched with a welt in it, that means that the needle must go through three thicknesses of hide. This might be difficult if it is thick moose hide to begin with.

She first sews the front panels on to the back piece at the shoulders. This done, she carefully sews the sleeves on to the two pieces at the arm holes.

The collar, of double thickness, is then sewn on, followed by the sewing of a 3-inch facing under the lapels. Pockets are sewn in place and the lining is added to the coat.

If Mary wants a more traditional look for the jacket, she makes fasteners of moose bone in lieu of buttons. These are held in place by small pieces of hide going through holes in the bone. And they are hooked to little hide loops to close the jacket.

A smoke-tanned moose hide jacket can get stiff if it is worn in the rain. But this stiffness can ordinarily be worked out in continued wearing *(58)*.

58. Mary wearing a typical Indian jacket.

The Tikinâgan and Other Items

Tikinâgan

Most of the crafts of the Woodland Indians were, of necessity, highly practical. With the exception of purely decorative work, everything the Algonquin made had a purpose.

A *tikinâgan* was very helpful to a mother and was used in a variety of ways. With a tumpline tied to it, she could carry her child around very conveniently, hang him from a peg or branch or use the *tikinâgan* as a portable cradle in the house or in the tent *(59)*.

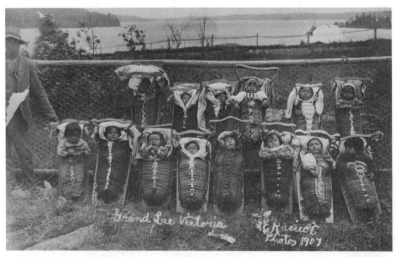

59. *Algonquin babies in their* tikinâgans *just as their parents are preparing to leave for the hunt. 1907.*
    Credit: National Museums of Canada

"Everyone made *tikinâgans* years ago," William says. "And not only that, the families used to pass their *tikinâgans* on to their neighbours. After they used it, they'd lend it. So one *tikinâgan* would serve maybe four or five families in the surrounding area. If you put the names on one *tikinâgan* of all the people who had used it in the old days, you'd have to have quite a list."

Ordinarily, the baby was put in the *tikinâgan* after he woke in the morning. Some babies slept loose at night; some could not sleep without being tied in the *tikinâgan*.

William says that after breakfast the baby might be crying, and if you gave him milk, he would still cry. But once he was tied in the *tikinâgan*, he would go to sleep. He would sleep two or three hours without moving at all. Around noon the mother would change the diaper and let the baby kick for a while, then the baby would be tied in for the afternoon. Later the mother most often took the baby out for the night.

If they travelled, the baby was kept in the *tikinâgan*. The protective brace over the baby's head helped insure against mishaps. A cheesecloth or other fly netting could be wrapped around the *tikinâgan* in the summer to keep mosquitoes and flies from the baby; the protective brace kept the netting from the baby's face.

In past days, diapers of moss were used. "In my day," William says, "we were already changing over to cloth diapers, although moss was still used sometimes. We didn't have Pampers in those days."

The *tikinâgan* is rarely seen today. Only in the more isolated reserves, such as Rapid Lake, certain places on James Bay and a few other areas, are the *tikinâgan* still in use. William and Mary's daughter-in-law used one for her children, but that was years ago and about the time the *tikinâgan* was disappearing around Maniwaki.

60. *Splitting* tikinâgan *back.*

To make a *tikinâgan,* William begins by splitting the back piece from a cedar block *(60).* Cedar was almost always used for the back in order that the *tikinâgan* be light for the woman to carry.

He splits out a board and begins to shape it. *Tikinâgans* had various dimensions, but generally they tapered from top to bottom. William's board is planed to a thickness of ¾ of an inch. The top is 14 inches wide and tapers to 11 inches wide at the bottom.

The brace that goes around to protect the head could be of ash, birch or black spruce. William prefers ash because it bends more easily. When craftsmen didn't have ash available they used other woods. William cuts a piece of ash 44 inches long. He then carves it until it is 1½ inches wide and ⅜ of an inch thick. As in bending the wood for other objects, he soaks the ash in water for a couple of days before steaming it. After it is steamed for a few minutes, he bends it to the desired shape. It is held in this shape by nails in a board until dry *(61).*

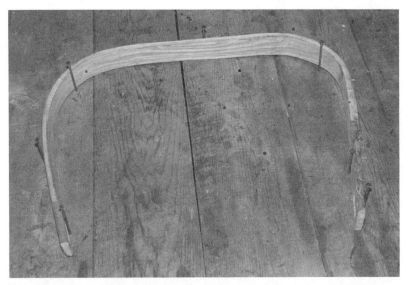

61. Bending the tikinâgan *brace.*

He then makes a notch in each side of the brace near the bottom *(62).* These two notches receive a cross-piece, 2 inches by 16 inches, that goes across the back of the *tikinâgan (63* and *64).* Fit then into the notches on the brace, this assembly is held in place on the back by three cord lashings through holes in the back piece and cross-piece. In the front, the brace is also held in place by cords coming up from the back piece.

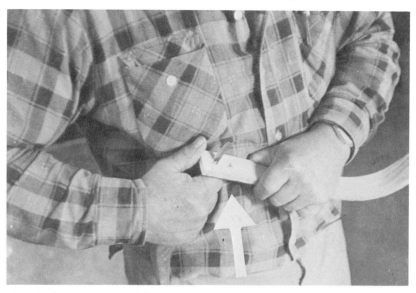

62. *Cutting slots in* tikinâgan *head brace.*

63. *Back piece of* tikinâgan.

64. *Fitting* tikinâgan *brace.*

The bottom board, to support the baby's feet, is made much the same way as the brace over the head. It is shaped until it is 38 inches long, 3½ inches wide and ⅜ of an inch thick, and tapered at both ends *(65)*. It is soaked, steamed and bent, and left until dry. Then it is held in place on the *tikinâgan* back board by four lashings through holes in the board and the foot rest *(66)*.

65. Carving tikinâgan *foot rest.*

66. Tikinâgan.

The Indian mother could carry a baby in a *tikinâgan* even while in a canoe *(67)*. The *tikinâgan* could be laid across two thwarts or it could be propped up on a rib and against a thwart, and the baby would then be facing the mother.

67. Doll illustrating how a tikinâgan *was used in a canoe.*

Moose Call

A moose call *(mônz potadjigan)* is used in the fall of the year for the moose hunt. An early Indian aid, they are now frequently used by

68. Moose call pattern.

white hunters as well. If the hunter is accustomed to using it, a series of muted grunts through the moose call can attract game.

In order to be worked properly, the bark for a moose call must either be fresh or soaked for some time prior to working with it.

Mary cuts the bark for a moose call from a very simple pattern *(68)*, approximately 20 inches high and 20 inches wide at the base. This can vary a little depending on what size moose call the hunter wants.

69. Scraping bark for moose call.

70. Folding moose call.

71. Pegging moose call.

72. Moose call with designs.

Loose bark is scraped from the white side of the sheet *(69)*. Then the sheet is folded with the white side of the bark on the inside of the call *(70)*.

Temporary wooden pegs are put into the seam with the aid of a small awl *(71)*. The moose call is then lashed along the seam with spruce root and can also be lashed on the circumference of the base of the call. The making of a moose call is therefore very much like the making of birchbark baskets.

If the moose call has been made from winter bark, designs are often added *(72)*.

Tumpline

The tumpline *(âpikan)* is an item that is little used today. A great boon to the Indians, it enabled them to carry heavy loads on their backs with less strain *(73)*.

73. *Carrying bark roll from woods with tumpline.*

White men quickly learned the use of the tumpline for the fur trade, but as the fur trade died out and the implements along with it, the use of the tumpline became more and more rare.

Ordinarily used by itself and tied around the burden, the tumpline was also occasionally sold affixed to canvas backpacks. These too have almost disappeared *(74)*.

The tumpline is of great benefit for the canoe carry and some canoeists still employ it. When tied and used properly, it enables the canoeist to alternate the weight of the canoe from the head to the shoulders so that he does not get tired out as quickly.

The tumpline is tied for the canoe carry with the canoe lying flat on the ground. After the paddles have been lashed to the thwarts so that they won't move, the tumpline is tied around the centre thwart. The tumpline should extend up from the thwart a distance equal to the

74. *Tumpline on backpack.*

distance between the canoeist's elbow and the base of his thumb *(75)*. The line is then left to drop through the paddles and later sits on the top of the head during the carry.

In tying a load to be carried on the back, the full weight should not be too high on the back but rather should rest in the area around the small of the back.

Mary no longer makes many tumplines but she made them often in the past. To cut the pieces for her tumpline, she first has a fully tanned, smoked moose hide. Because she wants the thickest hide for the tumpline, she cuts the headband of the tumpline from the neck of the hide. The headband is cut 2 feet long and 2¼ inches wide. Then she cuts the hide down the middle of the back. One of the straps is taken from the border of each half, always along the back. Each strap is ¾ of an inch wide, tapering to the ends, and 9 feet long *(76)*.

75. *Measuring tumpline length for carry.*

She sews about 3 inches of each strap on to the headband, as it has to support a heavy weight. In stitching the straps to the tumpline headband, Mary uses a round awl to make the holes and a heavy

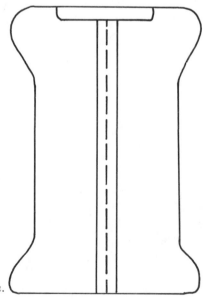

76. *Tumpline pattern.*

thread (or sinew in the old days) for the sewing. A triangular awl, although quite practical for work with birch bark, had a tendency to tear hide.

When not in use, the tumpline is rolled up. Leaving a loop of about 2 feet, by tying the ends together before the tumpline is completely rolled, allows it to be carried conveniently over the shoulder.

A tumpline should be oiled from time to time *(77)*. If the long straps on each side get dry, they break. And with the frequent heavy loads that the tumpline must support, breakage would come quickly.

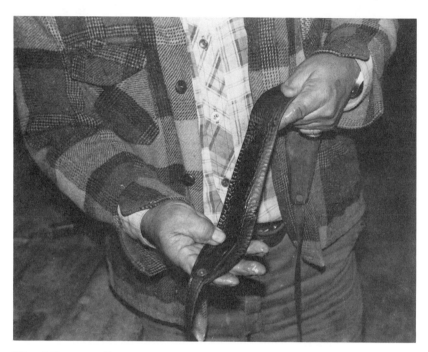

77. *Oiling tumpline.*

Drum

Drums were part of the ceremonial accoutrements of most of the Indian tribes of North America. The Algonquin are no exception to this, but like other tribes their use of the drum has diminished; even less common today is the making of the drum.

To make a drum, William selects a cedar log. In this case, the block he cuts off is 14 inches high and 15 inches in diameter. These dimen-

78. *Hollow log for cedar drum.*

sions can vary according to what type of drum he is making. He also has chosen a cedar whose middle has begun to decompose. This enables him to chisel out the middle more easily *(78).*

79. *Chiseling out cedar block for drum.*

He first takes the bark off the outside with a drawknife or a crooked knife. To give it a smooth finish he sands it.

Then he finishes hollowing out the middle with a chisel *(79)*, leaving the wall uniformly thick all around—just over ½ inch.

After the frame for the drum has been completed, William cuts a piece of rawhide from deer hide or from thin moose hide. The hide must be thin in order to permit better reverberation. Cut round, and still moist, the hide is then placed over the top of the frame *(80)*. He turns the drum upside down and then places another round piece of hide over the bottom. Then he cuts double slits every 3 inches in both pieces of hide to receive the lashing.

Having already cut *babiche* for the drum, he aligns the slits so that they are not opposite one another and lashes the two pieces of hide together over the frame of the drum. The hide stretches as it dries and tightens considerably. When it is completely dry, it is ready to be used *(81)*.

80. Cut hide draped over drum.

Pounding on a drum with the hands is an African practice, not a North American Indian one. To make a drum stick, William wraps a small piece of hide a number of times around the end of a stick about a foot long and binds the hide with a small length of cord.

81. Finished drum.

Construction of the Birchbark Canoe

". . . And the forest's life was in it,
All its mystery and its magic . . ."
　　　　　—*The Song of Hiawatha*, Henry Wadsworth Longfellow

What is the particular appeal of the birchbark canoe? It's hard to say; everyone's reaction is different. In his epic poem, Longfellow sang the praises of the birchbark canoe and its builder, Hiawatha.

There are few canoeists who are not smitten by the first birchbark canoe they see. Anyone who loves the grace of an ordinary canoe but has not been in a birchbark canoe is missing something. There is as much difference between a birchbark canoe and an aluminum canoe as there is between an aluminum canoe and a rowboat. This is not necessarily a difference of performance (the bark canoe has advantages as well as disadvantages over other types) but is rather one of feeling.

You might compare it to the difference between a frame shelter and a log cabin. The extra attention that a bark canoe may require allows you to know your craft and its constituent materials, materials which have come from the woods only days earlier. In addition, the birchbark canoe may be the most striking manifestation of the material culture of the North American Indian.

Some people have suggested that the slightly slower speed of a birchbark canoe over other types of canoes is a disadvantage. But is it really? One who is so concerned with this slight difference would probably be better off using a true white man's conveyance, such as a plane, or at least a boat with a motor. These are much faster than even the sleekest of the synthetic canoes. A recent writer, commenting upon the birchbark canoe, noted that it was built from its environment, and was visually of its environment. And so it is.

The birchbark canoe was the most important vehicle in the opening up of Canada, more important than ships, because there were no deep inland waterways, and more important than trains, which didn't pierce the continent until late in the nineteenth century. Before the coming of the Europeans the Indians had developed the craft, perhaps the most suitable for wilderness travel. For hundreds of years, where no other craft could go, the birchbark canoe went. Even today, although the birchbark canoe has virtually disappeared, its commercially made cousins are an important means of conveyance in the woodland areas of the continent.

The lightness of the canoes allowed them to be carried over portages, an absolute must in an area of many lakes and rivers. They could be as short as an 8-foot, one-man canoe for trapping, or they could be as long as a 36-foot fur trade canoe that could carry 2 tons of cargo *(82)*.

Occasionally, other bark than birch was used, but these almost always made for inferior canoes. Spruce bark did not have nearly the useful qualities of birch bark. Elm bark was occasionally used by some tribes, but it was so heavy that what resulted was more like a miniature barge than a canoe. And pity the poor soul who had to try to portage the thing.

82. Charlie Smith in an 8-foot Algonquin trapper's canoe.
Credit: Leonard Lee Rue III

In the usual generosity of nature, birch bark suitable for canoes is commonly found, across the continent, in areas where canoes are most needed. The upper limits of the heavily deciduous forest is reached above Maniwaki. Beyond that, pine, spruce, and other conifers predominate. For this reason, Maniwaki, Rapid Lake and Manouan, all in western Quebec, have continued to be centres for canoe building.

Good birch bark was such a valuable commodity that it became sought after in trade. Indians who lived in areas where good bark was found could barter it with Indians from areas where there was inferior bark or no bark at all. Some Hudson's Bay Company posts sold rolls of birch bark.

William sold two rolls of birch bark to the National Museums of Canada in 1978, intended for a Cree builder. The man was eighty years old and had poor eyesight. He had been hired to build a canoe in Ottawa. The transaction in some ways approximated the trading in bark from the old days. Indians, Algonquin particularly, traded birch bark to other Indians in areas where it was of poorer quality.

Language study books have a way of attempting to involve the culture in teaching the language. When the French missionaries did this years ago in books on the Algonquin language, they gave an intriguing glimpse into the life of the people. In the following sentences, part of a drill in conversation from a missionary grammar, it is clear how great a part the canoe played in the scheme of things:

"You're good at making canoes. Hurry up and make one."

"That's what I intend to do. I have bark for a canoe, good bark."

"I only need a small canoe for myself."

"I'll make you one then. How long do you need it?"

"Ten feet will be good enough."

"Here is your canoe. Do you like it?"

"Yes, I like it. But it's not yet gummed."

"I'll gum it tomorrow."

"The waves are dangerous. Water is coming in the canoe. There is a small island over there. Let's try to get to it."

"Let's make a fire before it rains."

"Pull the canoe farther up on shore so the wind doesn't take it away."

"Do you think the wind will stop us for long?"

"Tomorrow the wind may go down and we may be able to leave."

(From Abbé Cuoq's *Grammaire de la langue algonquine*.)

William and Mary Commanda have been making several birchbark canoes a year for a number of years. William's father was not a canoe maker but Mary's was. She learned much of the techniques of canoe making from her father, Charlie Smith, who was a well-known builder. He worked on canoes almost up to the time he died at the age of ninety-four.

Late in his life, after Mary's mother had died, Charlie Smith came to live with the Commandas on the reserve near Maniwaki. He never adjusted well to the life on the reserve, missing the free existence he had known up along the Gatineau River. One day, not long before his ninety-fifth birthday, Mary caught him leaving the house with his packsack on his back. She was surprised and asked where he was going. He said that he was going to die soon and that he wanted to die in peace, up on the old hunting and trapping territory where he had passed all his life. He was finally talked out of going, but two weeks later he died.

Birchbark canoes were much a part of the childhood of both William and Mary. Mary tells of the time her mother was paddling Mary and her younger brother across a lake up near Micomis. The children were both small. Part way across the lake, they came upon a deer swimming in the water. In those days, no one passed up a chance to get meat. All Mary's mother had in the canoe was a hatchet. She killed the deer with it and grabbed the antlers. Managing to keep the children under control, she paddled with one hand, held the deer with the other, and made her way up to the shore.

William first used the birchbark canoe with his father, going into the woods from the time he was twelve years old. His father had the canoe for more than thirty years, suggesting that there can be longevity in the craft. It was twelve-and-a half feet long and was used for trapping. It would hold William, his father, their beaver dog, a tent and traps as well as food. They'd go for a month and a half or two months at a time.

The reason so small a canoe would suffice for such travel was the skill and carefulness of William and his father. Indians are often seen to travel along the shore with a canoe rather than straight across an open lake. William and his father knew how fast a wind could come up and they planned accordingly, often not going on a lake in the middle of a day but starting in the morning when there is little wind. Later, after William had trapped for a few years with his father, he'd go out by himself, often spending six weeks trapping alone in the woods.

The two would make trips of a hundred miles back in the woods, taking two weeks to get to their trapping grounds. They'd trap as they went and when they killed a moose, they'd take time to dry the meat. They would sometimes make a trip out in mid-winter, leaving the canoe on their trapping grounds and travelling out on snowshoes. If a canoe had to be taken in or out of the woods in the winter, it was drawn out on a handsleigh. This was particularly true when someone wanted to have a spring hunt. Then they had to get a canoe up into the woods before the snow went.

A trapper working alone would often make himself a canoe only 9 or 10 feet in length. Needless to say, they were quite tippy. They say that the paddler had to part his hair in the middle. This type of canoe was often left behind and sheltered so that another trapper could make use of it.

A birchbark canoe builder was an extremely hard man to trap in the woods. When William was young, he heard a story about the resourcefulness of a local Algonquin named Frank Mongo. Frank was coming out of the woods from his trapline in the spring sometime around the year 1890. He had his entire family with him along with a whole catch of furs and some odds and ends. When they loaded the canoe with people and gear, the water came to not more than an inch below the gunwales. Frank told his wife to go on ahead, that he would build a canoe and then follow, but that he might not be along until the next day.

Having taken some of the baggage from the first canoe, Frank set to work. He had some nails, and as nails were often used to make the work on a canoe shorter, he availed himself of them. From his starting time of building the canoe, which was in the morning, he worked straight through until four o'clock the following morning and ended up with a very serviceable birchbark canoe that measured about 12 feet in length.

William says that in 1925, when there were around 325 Indians in the River Desert Band, there were more than twenty canoe-makers, the best known among them being Pete Dubé and Charlie Commanda. Now there are around 1000 Indians in the River Desert Band and William and Mary have been the only active canoe-makers in recent years.

William learned in large part from his uncle, André Cayer, who was a stern taskmaster. But his uncle told him that he would one day thank him for his rigorous lessons and William today appreciates the truth in that statement.

In 1975, William and Mary taught a class of fifteen Algonquin students in Amos, Quebec, in the craft and art of making a birchbark canoe. They divided the students into two groups, each of them heading one. One would go into the woods for two or three days to look for materials while the other would stay with the second group and teach a part of the process. They made twelve canoes that summer, ranging in length from 10 to 16 feet. They wanted to make canoes of different lengths to give the students a wider experience. "They already knew a lot about building," William says. "I knew because of the way they handled the crooked knives. They came with their own crooked knives."

William and Mary took pictures of that summer's teaching. In one photo, two of the students are in the water in a 10-foot canoe. The combined weight of the two men was 350 pounds. "And they still could have put their packs in there," William said. He says that they had to go 20 or 25 miles for the cedar, about 60 miles for the birch bark, and the spruce root was close by.

William and Mary made the canoe forms in Amos for the different sizes of canoes and then left the forms there so that the people could continue to use them.

The Commandas also constructed a canoe in Washington, D.C., in 1976 during the Bicentennial celebration. They began it in Maniwaki and finished it in front of the Washington Monument. William maintains that, "We only went there to demonstrate the making of a canoe. I didn't go to celebrate someone else's bicentennial."

Birchbark canoes the Commandas have made are housed in museum collections in Canada, the United States, Japan, Germany, Poland, and France.

A rather interesting renaissance took place at Maniwaki in the summer of 1979.

Jocko Carle and Basil Smith, Mary's brother, decided to get into the canoe making business. They had seen that the craft had been good to William and Mary and wanted to try it themselves.

It's more accurate to say that they wanted to try it again. Basil had helped on canoes with his father, Charlie Smith. And Jocko Carle was a skilled canoe maker of long standing.

Jocko made many canoes with his father and brother through the 1930s. In those years the going price was one dollar a foot. The three of them working together would sometimes turn out two or three canoes a week.

But Jocko had not made a canoe for thirty-five years—since sometime during the war, as he recalls it, when he was trapping with Michel Côté on the Coulonge River, 60 or 70 miles west of Maniwaki. They had gone spring trapping with a canvas canoe. The rivers were open but there was still snow on the ground.

They had a lot of gear, along with fur and meat from a moose they had killed. Before heading back, they had come upon a birch tree about 2 feet in diameter. Thinking that it would be a fine thing if they had another canoe, they set to work.

Because the ground was frozen and there was no reasonable way to get spruce root, they had to improvise. They used nails for the gunwales. To bind the bows and to lash the thwarts into the gunwales, they used *babiche* from the moose they had just killed, hide that they had also used to fix their snowshoes. In four days, they had a good 14-foot canoe. One man in each canoe, they made their way back to Maniwaki.

The technique of using *babiche* to bind a canoe was not a common one. The Indians knew that spruce root lasted longer, that small animals were not likely to nibble on it as they would *babiche*. However, Jocko's use of it with Michel Côté that 1942 spring on the Coulonge River suggests that *babiche* did have a place in the construction of a birchbark canoe—when a canoe had to be made to get back in the early spring during a time when spruce root was unavailable.

To build their canoe in the summer of 1979, Basil and Jocko retreated to Basil's trapping cabin at Rock Lake, about 60 miles north of Maniwaki. There were some skeptics who doubted their ability to make a canoe after such a long hiatus. Would they come back with a canoe full of nails and pitch? One that would be better suited to going around corners?

They surprised everyone. Jocko's master hands had not lost any of their ability in thirty-five years. The canoe was 14 feet long and beautiful. The bows lined up well; the ribs and the sheathing were smooth and well made and they had been fortunate enough to get a large sheet of bark that was in fine condition. To have retained the ability to make a canoe after such a long interruption was a feat in itself.

They found a buyer for the canoe within a few days of bringing it back. With this encouragement, they returned to Rock Lake to build two more canoes.

Western Quebec and the area around Maniwaki is a good one for birch bark *(wikwas)*. William and Mary make several forays a year into the woods to look for birch bark and other canoe materials. Not too many years ago, they could walk back in the woods several miles from town and get all the wood and bark they needed for a canoe. Eventually, through pressure from logging and the fact that so many builders took bark from the area, good birch trees got hard to find. Now the Commandas go as far as 100 miles into the woods to obtain the bark. William says, "It costs $500 just to get the materials for a canoe." Although the man is Algonquin, he frequently suggests a certain kinship with Paul Bunyan in his flair for exaggeration.

It follows that if you seek a birch tree of exceptional quality and size, when you finally find one you are overcome with a feeling of

*83. A standing canoe
    birch.*

awe. A large birch tree meant a lot to the Indians. They could make a canoe from its outer bark, tea from the inner bark, and paddles and snowshoe frames from the wood *(83)*.

Jocko and Basil one day went into the woods to bring back birch bark and came back with two very large rolls.

Both were long, over 18 feet, and wide—one exceptionally so. The largest roll was 6 feet wide and 19 feet long. They had 114 square feet of birch bark in a single roll. Unfortunately, this largest roll was not usable for a canoe. It was slightly drier than they would have liked and had cracked in a couple of places. They feared that the final placing of the ribs into the canoe would cause even more cracks.

(Out of curiosity one day I weighed a few rolls of birch bark. Two rolls, roughly of standard size—each large enough for a 14-foot canoe—weighed 25 and 26 pounds. The large piece described above weighed 71 pounds.)

When the Commandas go into the woods, their usual procedure is to pack up their camper truck and sometimes stay the night, sometimes return the same day. William drives along a bush road until he spots the top of a large birch tree from the road. Usually he has already visited the area and knows that there are good birch trees in the vicinity. He parks the truck and gathers his gear for the walk back to the tree to examine it. At a minimum, he and Mary usually take back a saw, a couple of axes to peel the bark and a tumpline to wrap it up and carry it.

In order to build a birchbark canoe of 14 feet, William looks for a tree that has a minimum diameter of 15 inches at the butt. Even that doesn't guarantee the sheet of bark would be wide enough. He and Mary often have to sew smaller pieces on each side to increase the width.

But there are other things to consider. Just because the tree is large enough doesn't mean it can be taken. The trunk has to be as nearly straight as possible, or else when the longitudinal cut is made on the bark the sheet is twisted and unusable. Any knots that might be hidden in the bark would inevitably show up later in the canoe as bumps. William believes that his ancestors had a way of cutting a straight piece of bark from an arched trunk; he himself doesn't know how this might have been done.

The outer part of the birch is composed of several layers of bark. It is only the top layer which is white. The white outer layer is almost always inside of whatever article is made of birch bark.

The layer next to the tree, the cambium, is the growth layer of the tree and is also the layer that gives dark colouring to the inner bark in the early part of the year.

Before any real effort is made, the bark has to be tested. William taps the axe blade into the bark at a lower level and takes off a small piece of bark to examine it.

For use in a canoe, birch bark must be of a minimum thickness. Strangely, it would be possible to find a birch tree 2 feet in diameter whose bark was too thin. William, already having made sure the trunk is straight, checks for thickness of the bark. If he finds that the bark is ⅛ of an inch thick or more, the bark passes that test.

84. Testing bark for suppleness.

If the bark is diseased he can't take it. He also checks for pliability. Birch bark is made up of a number of layers. In healthy bark, these layers stay together. If the bark is of poor quality, the layers separate and the bark must be rejected. The test for this is simply to bend the sample piece of bark back and forth. When the bark is folded, outside in, it resists cracking *(84)*. One type of bark at first resembles winter bark. It is called red bark *(miskwa wikwas)* and is very prone to cracking.

Before he fells the tree, William makes a solid bed on which the tree can land. The bed is nothing more than a cradle of small trees placed a little above the point where the lower branches of the birch tree will fall. If the trunk of the birch tree is not thus prevented from hitting the ground as it falls, it often hits a rock or a tree stump, thus damaging the bark. This would produce an ugly hole in the middle of the canoe, or render the bark useless entirely.

In prehistoric times, it was hard to fell a tree. Fire accomplished the task. The Indian first applied wet mud around the bark he wished to be preserved. Then he built a good fire at the base of the trunk. When the wood below the mud was charred, he chopped away the burnt part with a crude stone axe. He repeated the steps until he had cut through the trunk entirely.

When William and Mary have the tree down, they make a cut from the base of the trunk to the spot where the branches begin. This cut is about ½ inch deep—just enough to cut through the bark. From that point they try to peel the bark from the trunk along its entire length at the same pace. The hand is pushed between the bark and the tree to

85. Starting to peel bark.

help remove the bark. Sometimes a dull-pointed wooden wedge is used to pry it off. And a stick, 8 or 10 feet long, may be used to roll against the trunk to insure that the bark comes off evenly *(85, 86, and 87)*. If the cutting is done on a warm day, the bark comes off easily. In colder weather the bark is much harder to remove. It's then that special care has to be taken to avoid tearing the bark. Sometimes, especially in winter, boiling water would have to be applied to the trunk before the bark could be peeled.

86. Jocko Carle peeling birch bark.

87. Peeling bark.

When the bark is off, it is one large sheet about 16 feet long and 4 feet wide, the size varying greatly, of course, according to the size of the tree.

The bark is rolled up with the outside of the bark (the white side) on the inside of the roll *(88)*. The roll is then tied with a tumpline and carried off *(89)*.

88. Rolling bark.

89. Tying bark roll with tumpline.

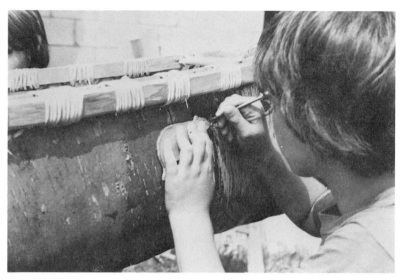

90. Making designs on canoe.

91. Scraping designs on bark.

William and Mary try to get winter bark when they can. This name, *pipon wikwas* in Algonquin, is given to bark that is removed with the dark, innermost layer of bark. This is so highly prized because when wetted, the dark layer can be scraped away. Figures in silhouette can be drawn on a canoe finished with winter bark *(90* and *91)*. Beaver and moose are the figures the Commandas most commonly draw on the canoes they make. A stencil is applied to the winter bark and then the surrounding moist bark is scraped off, leaving a dark figure on the hull.

Summer bark is uniformly light and doesn't lend itself to the making of these designs.

Birch bark is a light, water-tight, and wonderfully resilient material. It is still pliable when removed from the tree but it dries within days, becoming hard and brittle to a certain degree. It's invariably in the roll by this time. However, a roll of birch bark can be saved for many months, if conserved in the proper place, and then be put to good use. Bark must be completely soaked for days before it returns to pliability. A birchbark canoe that is in the water from time to time is a healthy canoe. The bark absorbs a little water and more or less breathes again.

Probably the hardest part of the construction of a birchbark canoe is gathering the materials—in particular, knowing where and how to gather them.

For a fastener, the only thing that holds a birchbark canoe together is lashing with the root of the spruce tree. This root, called *watap* by the Algonquin, is fairly easy to gather, but in its preparation and lash-

92. *Pulling spruce root from ground.*

93. Tying roots.

ing, it represents perhaps one-third of the time involved in building a birchbark canoe.

To get *watap*, William and Mary go to a place 100 miles northeast of Maniwaki. Here 30-foot spruce trees grow in fairly open areas. Therefore, not only do these trees have long roots, but the roots are not entangled with the roots of the surrounding underbrush—which doesn't mean that they are not entangled with each other.

Mary goes a few feet out from the trunk of a spruce tree and digs down with a pointed stick. A dull point on a stick gets through the dirt but does not damage the roots *(92)*.

When she locates a good root, she tears out its whole length, which often approaches 20 feet. Often the root on which she is tugging crosses under another root. She then feeds it under and continues, also leaving another root to work on when she finishes with the first.

When she has a number of roots piled one upon the other, she rolls them up like a doughnut and ties the roll *(93)*. This 20-pound doughnut can then be carried out of the woods conveniently.

The very few parts of the canoe that are not water-tight are sealed with spruce gum *(pĭkiw)*. In spring when the sap flows up the trees, the spruce gum can be gathered in nearly the same way as maple sap. At other times of the year, it has to be scraped laboriously from wounds in spruce trees.

To get cedar for ribs, gunwales and sheathing, William goes about 80 miles west of the place where he and Mary have earlier harvested the spruce root.

Proper cedar for ribs and sheathing is not difficult to find. William needs logs only 4 or 5 feet in length.

White cedar is notoriously knotty and its grain twisty. A finished rib should not have a knot in it. Even a small knot causes the wood to curve around it. A twisted grain does not split straight. These logs can be had in almost any cedar grove.

What is hard to come by though, and is the reason for William's going once again 100 miles or more into the woods, is the fine, straight, long cedar log that is used for the gunwales. Here, the search for long cedar is akin to the search for good bark.

You could count ten thousand birches before finding one that would serve for a canoe. Likewise, you could search among hundreds of white cedar before finding one whose trunk was clear of knots, whose bark indicated a straight grain and whose length measured 16 feet.

William has his own stand of cedar sequested far away in the woods. He approaches a likely tree, puts his hand on the trunk and walks around it once or twice, head upraised to examine the trunk.

He then fells the tree and cuts off a log just below the branches. He splits the log in half using steel and hardwood wedges and a 5-pound hammer or an axe *(94)*. And he again splits the wood, so that quarters remain, each of them 16 feet long. If the quarters are of medium size, they might yield four gunwales—enough for one canoe. With two or three big cedar trunks, William stocks up on enough long cedar to make many canoes.

94. Splitting cedar log.

An illustration of William's gift for embellishment occurred precisely during one of these sessions of splitting a cedar log into quarters for the gunwales.

At the top of one log was a square hole that looked as though it had been pecked into the wood by a woodpecker. However, it was as square as could be and had three of us examining it closely and completely. William asked, "Either of you see this before?" We hadn't. "I've never in my life seen a bird make a hole like that," he said.

Now William has a good knowledge of Algonquin culture—and what he doesn't know, he makes up. He was scheduled, a few weeks thence, to give a talk at a museum in New York state. He studied the square hole in the log for a few more moments and finally said thoughtfully, "You know, I should cut this out of the log and take it to the museum with me. I could talk all morning on this."

These first steps in building the birchbark canoe are the most difficult; gathering the material is a very big part of the entire job. You might almost say that worthy canoe birch and white cedar do not grow on trees, so hard are they to find.

Before actual construction of the canoe, the materials that have been gathered have to be prepared. The big roll of birch bark is submerged in water for a few days, so that it will be pliable. If it is not soaked, it becomes so brittle that it is unusable.

The preparation of the spruce root is a simple but long job. Ideal root is the diameter of a pencil. The root is also soaked for a time so that it is easier to work with. Wet, the thin bark covering the root comes off easily.

Then a split is started at one end of the root with a little knife cut *(95)*. The root is evenly split for its length, which may be as long as 15 or 20 feet. If the split starts to run to one side, the other root half is pulled until the split evens up *(96)*.

95. Starting root split.

96. Splitting root.   *97. Boiling root.*

There is a thin bark that must be removed from the spruce root and boiling is sometimes necessary to facilitate this. A good time to do this is after the root has been split in half *(97)*. It is then easily peeled with the thumbnail. There are often tiny branches on the root which should be removed at this time as well.

Once this length of root is split all the way, both halves are sometimes split again to be rid of the middle (a coarser fiber) of the root.

98. A prepared roll of watap.

After a long root is split, it is again rolled into a coil. It can then be left to dry if desired and soaked once again before it is to be used *(98)*. In fact, once gathered, the materials used in the building of a birchbark canoe can be left to dry indefinitely. All that is necessary to get them in top shape again is to soak them in water. The versatility of the primary materials the Indians used never ceases to amaze.

For William and Mary's construction of a canoe, the old Indian tools in most cases suffice. William splits the cedar gunwales by hand because the split is stronger if it follows the grain. Likewise, ribs and sheathing are hand-split.

William has five or six crooked knives and about the same number of drawknives. These two hand tools are no longer common; it's hard to buy them today. But they are extremely useful.

The drawknife is an old settler's tool. It is nothing more than a straight blade with handles on each end, perpendicular to the blade. The carver pulls the blade towards himself. This used to be very often employed for taking bark from logs. William uses it to make paddles and snowshoe frames and for finishing gunwales, ribs, and sheathing after they have been split. It is not easy to use a drawknife at first, but the knack is gotten with a little practice. The beginner has a tendency to pull the knife toward him so the blade is at right angles to the line of pull; the correct method is to pull the knife in a straight line but with the blade at an angle. The cutting is smoother this way. The carver also takes time to become sensitive to each movement of the blade in order to work with precision. Those who take the time to learn to use the drawknife swear by it.

The crooked knife is an old Indian tool. Its appearance and method of use roughly approximate those of a hunting knife that would be pulled toward the carver. However, the handle is bent away, allowing the thumb to be braced against it. And the blade is slightly curved. The knife is pulled towards the carver because this action, as in the case of the drawknife, gives more control. The crooked knife also requires habituation, but once the carver has acquired it, he finds this a very useful tool. It is also more versatile than the drawknife, being able to carve in close spots.

How closely the crooked knife is associated with the Indian can be illustrated in an interesting way. In the Maniwaki area, there are a number of Indians and a number of white men who make axe handles and paddles. Despite long years of association with each other, the white men invariably use the drawknife for this work while the Indians use the crooked knife.

In aboriginal times, the tools were much more primitive. Holes in the bark were made with a triangular bone awl. Holes in wood were made using a type of awl with a bow that made it rotate. In fact, it looked much like the assembly the Indians used for making a fire. And when the ribs were split they were finished by means of abrasion, not by cutting as is done today. Indians used stones or shells to wear down the ribs, gunwales, and sheathing to proper form. Whatever the tools used, the Indian built a craft of remarkable workmanship, even in prehistoric times.

If the Indian benefitted from the use of steel tools, the coming of the white man brought a bastardization to the construction of the birchbark canoe. As early as the nineteenth century, it was common to see gunwales and gunwale covers held together by nails. It is not hard to understand why; nails saved a lot of labour. Binding gunwales with spruce root was very time-consuming, although spruce root was no less effective than nails. William and Mary favour spruce root because it makes for a much more attractive canoe.

The birchbark canoe formerly was constructed on the ground and under a canopy made of saplings and birch bark sheets, to keep the sun out. (Birch bark dries after a while and cannot be worked unless it is very pliable, as has already been mentioned.) The old canoe bed was made on ground that was soft enough to accept wooden stakes and solid enough to hold them.

In the last century or so, building platforms have become common. In this way, several canoes could be constructed with a minimum of inconvenience.

A building platform is made by joining boards together. This platform is about 4 feet wide and 16 feet long, depending upon the size of the canoe, and reproduces the canoe bed that had formerly been laid on the ground. Building a canoe on a platform rather than on the ground has no effect, necessarily, on the form or structure of the finished canoe.

William sets his platform up on carpenter's horses so that it isn't necessary to kneel down while working on the canoe. Holes he drills in the platform receive the stakes that hold up the sides of the canoe.

These holes are placed along the gunwale line about a foot and a half apart, and are always directly across the canoe from the stake on the opposite side.

After the roll of bark has been soaked for several days, it is unrolled, exterior side up, on the building platform *(99)*. Loose bark is pulled off the sheet. The bark William and Mary use for this canoe is cut to 13½ feet. (Measurements given here are for a 13-foot canoe. For longer canoes, they would be increased proportionately.) In forming the bow later on, a few inches will have to be trimmed from each end. Only ⅛ of an inch thick, this bark is thinner than usual. And its narrow width of 34 inches means that more bark than usual will have to be sewn on the sides.

99. Unrolling birch bark to begin construction.

All during the building process boiling water is kept at the ready. It is frequently poured over the birch bark and the cedar to make them more pliable.

When the bark is spread out on the platform, a plywood frame is centred on top of it and is weighted down with heavy stones *(100)*. The frame is 30 inches wide and 12 feet long. The frame is roughly the same size as the inwales and is used to form the bottom of the canoe. Some builders use the inside gunwales for this purpose and later raise the gunwales to their final position.

When the bark is well weighted-down, seven gores are cut on each side of the bark and the sides are turned *(101)*. These gores are about a foot and a half apart, corresponding in position to the stakes in the building platform, and with the middle gores at the central thwart. William and Mary always overlap the gores in the same direction, so that they are streamlined from the bow to the stern. It is this overlap-

100. Bark weighted down under building frame.

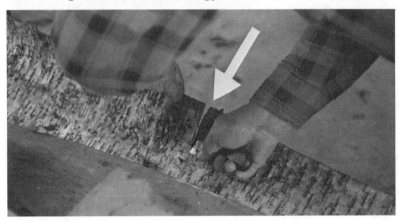

101. Cutting gore in side of canoe.

ping from the same direction that gives a birchbark canoe a bow and a
stern, although both ends of the canoe look the same to those unfa-
miliar with birchbark canoes. Some builders, however, overlapped
from both ends to the middle, so that the gores were streamlined no
matter how the canoe was headed.

Should there be a tear in the side of the bark already, it is often
used as a gore. The purpose of the gore is to give a proper shape to
the canoe. Without the gores, the canoe would be hogged, that is, the
centre of the canoe would be higher than the two bows.

Some builders then sewed the gores. William and Mary do not, as
their bark is held together by virtue of the bark's being solidly
pinched between the inwale and the outwale. At this point the sides of

the canoe are first raised and the sides are also staked at the same time *(102)*.

The inwale frame is pre-assembled, tied at the ends and held apart by dummy thwarts. The dummy centre thwart is 28 inches long, the middle ones are 23 inches long and the small end ones are 8 inches long *(103)*.

102.   Tying stakes to hold the sides up.

103.   Dummy centre thwart in frame.

For this canoe, the inwale measures 1 inch by ⅝ inch (on top) at the middle thwart and tapers to ⅝ inch by ½ inch (on top) at the inside of the bow where the two inwales are joined. The bottom edge of the inwale nearest the bark is beveled to receive the ribs later on. The inwale is also measured off in 2-inch intervals where the spruce root lashing and rib placements alternate *(104)*. The outwale measures 1¼ inches by ½ inch (on the top side) and tapers to ¾ inch by ⅜ inch at the end.

The inner gunwale frame and the outwales are then put in place. Then hardwood stakes are put into their holes to hold the sides of the

104. Markings along gunwale to determine placement of lashing and ribs.

105. Pouring hot water on bark to facilitate forming of bow.

canoe up and to hold the gunwales in place. A piece of old sheathing is placed inside the stakes to help support the bark. At this time, William and Mary work together to clamp the two bows temporarily *(105)*. Even at this early forming of the bows, they try to keep them well aligned.

Stakes are put inside the canoe. Planted against the frame on the bottom, they are tied to the outside stakes. The assembly now has the approximate form of a canoe.

To form the rocker of the Algonquin canoe, William slides a long wedge beneath the bow *(106)*. This wedge lifts each bow.

106. Wedge under bow for lift.

107. Measuring stick for proper gunwale height.

William makes some adjustments with a measuring stick *(tipahigans)* to make sure that the gunwales are the proper height, both amidships and at the bows *(107)*. Then he fastens them into place with temporary clamps *(108)*.

108. Gunwales clamped temporarily in place.

109. Trimming the bark down to the gunwales.

The bark is trimmed almost even with the tops of the gunwales *(109)*. William is trying something a little different with this canoe. He is overlapping the bark on the inwale. Often when the ribs are placed in the canoe, they cause the inwale to ride up so that it is half an inch higher or so than the outwale. Neither the *watap* lashing nor the wooden pegs in the gunwales seem to stop this riding up. With the bark lapped over the inwale, this problem should be stemmed.

110. Putting pegs in gunwales.

Before sewing the spruce root, a square hardwood peg *(mitikötcita-haskwan)* is driven through the inwale and outwale at each lashing location *(110)*. Later the lashing will hide the pegs.

Mary is in charge of sewing the gunwales. At each spot that must be bound, she makes four holes with a small awl *(mîkos)* through the bark, just below the gunwales. Then a single length of spruce root is passed around the gunwales eight times, twice through each hole *(111)*. When each section is finished, the bark is sandwiched very tightly between the two cedar gunwales. It is more tightly bound than if nails had been used. It would take a lot less force to pull the gunwales apart with nails in them than it would when they are bound with spruce root.

111. Sewing the gunwales.

Spruce root stretches very slightly when wet so that it dries tight. It's an extremely useful material. The more time spent in the preparation of the *watap*, the better the finished job. Not only do good builders make sure the root is strong, but they see to it that the *watap* is even and, particularly, that it is sewn evenly. Some of the finest builders even varied the width of the *watap* lashing along the gunwale, more for looks than anything else. (I use the past tense because these men are now gone.) But it is another attestation to the painstaking work that a builder put into his canoe.

There are perhaps fifty or sixty intervals along the gunwales that require binding. This takes up much of the total time involved in making a canoe.

Mortises are cut into the inwales with a chisel to receive the thwarts *(pîmitisa)*. When William puts the mortise into the inwale for the centre thwart, the mortise goes only as deep as the bark, not through the bark. He is always careful to have the lashings on both sides of the mortise site finished before making it, as the lashing will prevent a split in the inwale from spreading, should one occur *(112)*.

The thwart then goes through the inwale only as far as the sand-wiched bark and is lashed in place with spruce root. The paddler in an Indian canoe kneels in front of the thwart and leans back against it; therefore a thwart, to support the weight, should not be made of cedar but rather of a hardwood.

After the small thwarts near the bow are lashed, the building frame is removed from the canoe. (The frame can be taken out because the middle thwart has not been lashed in place; William has only nailed it temporarily.)

112. Making mortise for centre thwart.

113. Splitting ribs with froe.   *114. Splitting ribs.*

The ribs *(wâgina)* are formed by first splitting the cedar log in quarters. Then the heartwood is split away. William splits the remaining piece in half with a froe, always starting at the small end of the log and going towards the butt end *(113)*. Should a split begin to go off to one side, that side is kept as straight as possible while the thick side is bent away more sharply *(114)*. He splits until he gets the rough form of the rib—roughly ⅜ of an inch thick and 2 inches wide. In splitting the cedar for ribs, great care is taken to split precisely, so that the two broad sides do not have to be carved later with the drawknife. In this way, the ribs are smooth and do not show the carving strokes. He then finishes the ribs with a drawknife, on a carving horse. Shaped something like a carpenter's horse, the carving horse has an arm in the centre that holds the wood so both hands can be used on the drawknife. Alternately, the rib can be finished with the crooked knife *(mokotâgan) (115)*.

The ribs are notched to distinguish the butt end from the top end. Butt ends and top ends are alternated because tensile strength varies, being stronger near the butt. Alternating ends distributes the tensile strength. Extra ribs are made in case any should be damaged or broken in the building process. William makes a bundle of the ribs and soaks them several days in water before using them. There were thirty-six ribs in this canoe.

The quality of the work in a birchbark canoe can be determined in a number of ways. One of the main ones is to examine the finish of the ribs. A builder who has taken great care in the making of the ribs has

115. Finishing a rib.

116. Splitting sheathing.

finished the surfaces of the ribs so that they are almost perfectly smooth, something that might seem difficult with a crooked knife but is well within the reach of the master builder. Other wooden parts should also be as smooth as possible. Pieces that still show the splitting, or pieces that have too many knife marks, are the work of a less competent builder. Once one has seen a number of birchbark canoes, he finds the skill of the really good builder amazing.

The sheathing *(apisidaganik)* is more thinly split than the ribs and is also two to three times as wide *(116)*. These pieces are also soaked in water so that they will be easier to work with later.

When the gunwales are sewn to their entire length with spruce root, the Commandas begin the work of forming the bows.

117. Lifting inwales up to proper height with temporary headboard.

118. The split stem-piece.

The first step in forming the bow is to raise the ends of the inwales. William wets the inwales with hot water to make them easier to bend. The water is applied for a couple of feet near the bow where most of the bending is going to be done. The inwale bow is then raised from 5 inches off the tip of the building frame to 10 inches off the building frame. It is then held in place with a support *(117)*.

William fashions a triangular piece of cedar about 3 feet long, to be the stem-piece *(wâginawinj)*. This he splits partially four times, leaving it unsplit at one end *(118)*. The piece is split so that it will be easier to bend. He then steams the piece for a few minutes, bends it to the bow curvature he wants and ties it in that shape to dry with a basswood strip *(119)*. The other stem-piece is bent the same way, care being taken to bend the second stem-piece to the same curvature as the first *(120)*.

119. William bending stem-piece.

120. Mary using basswood strip to bind stem-piece after bending.

121. Splitting outwale to bend it up for the bow.

122. Bending outwale end.

When the stem-pieces are dried in form, William and Mary fit them to the bows and clamp them temporarily in place. After the stem-piece is sewn in, the gunwale ends are bent slightly up and joined to it *(121)*. In most canoes, the upper sweep of the gunwale ends is such that laminations have to be made to aid the bending. The gunwales are split three or four times back to the first lashing at the end thwart, or about 14 inches from the tip of the gunwale. When bending the gunwale ends upward, William and Mary apply hot water to them with a dipper *(122)*.

Then, a little back from the bow, a headboard *(otinimanganikadjigan,* i.e., shoulder device) is added. It is of cedar, 12 inches high and 4 inches wide, with a thickness of ¾ of an inch *(123)*. This shoulders the two gunwales and is based on the bottom end of the stem-piece, giving added support. (It is interesting to note that the Algonquin word for this support piece is more closely related to its function than are the two commonly used English words—headboard and manboard.)

123. Carving headboard.

124. Bow stitching.

William cuts the bark of the bow to the curvature he wants. It is this bow design that is the most important characteristic distinguishing the canoes of one tribe from the canoes of another. The Ojibwa had a bow that was greater than a semi-circle, tumbling home towards the stern. The Algonquin stem-piece in most models points roughly straight up. Some tribes had variations of their own. A low bow might be employed where the canoeist wanted to go along streams with overhanging branches. Or they may have been made to avoid taking too much wind on open lakes. Also, although they generally stuck fairly close to their traditional pattern, different builders within the same tribe had various ways of making a bow. One canoe-maker's work usually could be easily recognized by another canoe-maker.

After William has cut the bark of the bow, Mary's work begins again. She sews the cedar stem-piece to the bark with spruce root, and her careful stitching makes a very decorative bow *(124)*. The bow is reinforced by lashing the two gunwales together just inboard of the stem-piece.

When the bows are finished, the canoe is nearing completion. The hull is shaped, the gunwales are in place and bound with spruce root, the ends are finished and cut a fine figure. Three operations remain: the ribs and sheathing have to be placed in, the gunwale covers have to be pegged to the gunwales, and the whole canoe has to be gummed.

Ideally, all the parts of a canoe should be pre-finished. Before anything is joined together, the spruce root should be prepared and the ribs and sheathing split and laid out. Then when construction begins, the operation isn't much more than a process of fitting things together.

William puts the final touches on the ribs and Mary tapers the pieces of sheathing with a knife *(125)*. They are then submerged in water again to make them less brittle and easier to use.

When it's time for the ribs to go into the canoe, two are taken at a time and placed abeam across the gunwales *(126)*. A line is traced on the rib at the inside of the inwale on each side of the canoe. William uses a piece of wood that is the width of three fingers to draw these lines. It is at these two points that the two ribs will be bent.

For insertion into the canoe, the ribs are steamed, two at a time, for about five minutes. The old way of preparing the ribs is to soak them

125. Tapering sheathing.

126. Measuring ribs for bending.

for several days, then to pour boiling water over them at the two points where they are to be bent. William has constructed an 8-foot long box of sheet metal which is heated electrically. Putting water in the box and heating it up allows him to steam ribs in five minutes with less bother.

It should be pointed out that these are non-traditional ways of constructing a traditional birchbark canoe.

The use of a steel knife, awl, carpenter's saw or steaming box is not traditional. Nor is felling a tree with a saw, for that matter. However, one may still end up with a traditional canoe, as these implements may not change workmanship, only make the work easier.

By contrast, employing nails to fasten the inwale and outwale together and hold down the gunwale cover, and pitch to seal the seams in the bark results in a birchbark canoe with significant non-traditional elements.

Ribs that William puts into this canoe are 2¼ inches wide and ⅜ of an inch thick. Length varies according to the position in the canoe. After the ribs are steamed, they are bent with the knee in the two marked places *(127)*.

127. Bending ribs.

Temporary sheathing is put into the canoe to duplicate the depth of the real sheathing. Then the ribs are fitted into the canoe *(128)*. When one rib is bent with another, the two ribs can be set amidships in the canoe and the rib on top can be moved closer to the bow. The canoe narrows toward the bows so the rib, which had been inside the other one, fits very well. After the set of two ribs is fitted into the canoe as snug against the bottom as it will go, it is left there. If it has a tendency to pop out, the set of ribs is clamped to the gunwale on each side. Frequently the final rib before the bow is broken, to conform to the V-shape of the bow profile.

After all the ribs are fitted into the canoe, they are left there to dry *(129)*. For this temporary fitting of the ribs, a binder is put in the canoe. Two pieces about the dimensions of the gunwales are put in the bottom of the canoe and then cross braces are wedged against them, forcing the ribs to stay in place. Under the thwarts 6-inch sticks

128 and 129. Placing ribs in canoe.

of wood are also wedged in to keep the binder toward the bottom of the canoe *(130)*.

When dry, the ribs can be taken out and laid aside, while the sheathing is carefully placed, overlapping, to cover the entire inner hull right up to the gunwales. Once the sheathing is put in the bow, it is fitted past the headboard all the way to the stem-piece on the inside

130. Ribs held in place with binder.

131. Placing sheathing in bow of canoe.

(131). In this way the sheathing gives extra protection for that section of bark between the headboard and the stem-piece.

The rib ends are carved to fit perfectly under the inner gunwale and are then fitted back in over the sheathing *(132)*. William places the ribs in the canoe starting from the centre thwart and going toward the bow.

132. Finishing rib ends.

With the wooden mallet, the rib is tapped nearly into place. The ribs are all tapped in at an angle at first so that excess pressure is not exerted at any single spot. Going to the bow once or twice, the ribs are tapped into an upright position as simultaneously as possible to distribute the pressure on the bark.

133. Pegging gunwale cover.

When this is done, William fits the gunwale cover *(apatapikâhigan)*—almost like a cedar gunwale turned on its side—over the two gunwales. The gunwale cover is a protection for the spruce root lashing. It is slightly hollowed on the bottom to receive the spruce root. He secures them in place using square hardwood pegs driven into the gunwales *(133)*.

The pegs are left in overnight in the gunwale cover to allow for a little drying. The next day they are pounded in further, if need be, and cut off. They may then be sanded or carved to make a smooth finish on the gunwale cover.

It is quite common, in recent canoes, to see nails used instead of spruce root, to hold the inwale and outwale together, as it often happened that the gunwale cover was held in with nails. Neither was necessary, but the traditional way demanded much more skill—and time.

There remains at this stage a little finishing work to be done on the canoe. This is a sort of polishing wherein any mistakes are noted and corrected; it also includes a go-round of the canoe with the crooked knife. Square edges of ribs are rounded slightly as are the square edges of gunwale covers *(134)*.

134. Smoothing edges of ribs.

When a birchbark canoe is completed to this point, it is reasonably impervious to water. It is necessary, however, to seal it completely with spruce gum.

135. Melting spruce gum and fat.

Pieces of hard gum are gathered from wounds in spruce trees, and it takes a great deal of gathering, because the builder might get very little from a single tree. Once he has a nice panful, William melts it down and then skims the impurities (dirt or flecks of wood) from the surface *(135).* Then fat and often powdered charcoal are added to the

136. Gumming seams of canoe.

gum as tempering agents. The former is added so that the gum will be elastic enough not to crack, and the latter is added so that the mixture will not run unduly in the sun.

Then the gum is applied on the two ends, at all seams and at any points along the hull where it appears that there might be a small hole. When this gumming is done, the canoe is finished *(136)*. The canoe that William and Mary constructed is 13 feet, 4 inches long, 33 inches in the beam, and 13½ inches deep; it weighs 52 pounds.

Sometimes it happened that the canoe needed a bit of additional gumming while in the woods. Often the canoeist carried a small tin gum pot hung by a short wire in the bow of the canoe. This pot contained gum that had already been tempered. And because it had hardened in the pot, it couldn't fall out. If a leak developed in the canoe, the pot would be put over a little fire, the gum melted and then a little applied to the spot on the canoe. The remainder then hardened again in the pot.

If the traveller had not brought a gum pot along, he could take a few hard knobs of spruce gum directly from a tree. These he chewed well until they were soft, then applied to the canoe.

William tries out his canoe by taking it to a lake for a trial run. He pays careful attention to the bottom of the canoe to see if there are any leaks. If he notices one, he takes the canoe up on shore, turns it over and finds the leak by sucking air where he thinks it might be *(137)*. When he finds the leak, which is probably in an area that has already been gummed, he lights a match or a small piece of birch bark

137. Checking for air hole in gum.

138. Melting a little gum on canoe to close over small leak.

139. William and Mary with the canoe, here near completion.

to melt a little of the surrounding gum, and then seals the leak *(138)*.

With proper care, there is no reason that a birchbark canoe cannot last as long as the person who owns it *(139)*.

Bibliography

The following list is offered for those interested in further reading on aspects of Algonquin culture discussed in this book.

ADNEY, EDWIN TAPPAN. "How an Indian Birchbark Canoe is Made." *Harper's Young People* (July 29, 1890), Supplement.

ADNEY, EDWIN TAPPAN and CHAPELLE, HOWARD I. *The Bark Canoes and Skin Boats of North America*, Smithsonian Institution, Bulletin No. 230. Washington: U.S. Government Printing Office, 1964.

ANDRÉ, LOUIS. *Dictionnaire Algonquin*. Oka, Quebec: manuscript, 1688?

ANONYMOUS MISSIONARY. *Dictionnaire Algonquin-Français de l'an 1661*. Oka, Quebec: manuscript, 1661.

ANONYMOUS MISSIONARY. *Dictionnaire Français-Algonquin*. Oka, Quebec: manuscript, 1662?

ANONYMOUS MISSIONARY. *Dictionnaire Français-Algonquin*. Oka, Quebec: manuscript, 1669.

ANONYMOUS MISSIONARY. *Aiamie-Tipadjimowin Masinaigan*. Montréal: J. M. Valois, 1890.

ASSINIWI, BERNARD. *Recettes indiennes*. Montréal: Leméac, 1972.

ASSINIWI, BERNARD. *Survie en forêt*. Montréal: Leméac, 1972.

CAMP, MIKE. *Recreating the Birchbark Canoe*. Cobalt, Ontario: Highway Book Shop, 1977.

CUOQ, JEAN-ANDRÉ. "Grammaire de la Langue Algonquine." *Mémoires de la Société Royale du Canada* (Section I, 1891).

CUOQ, JEAN-ANDRÉ. *Lexique de la langue algonquine*. Montréal: J. Chapleau et fils, 1886.

DEAN, JEFF. "Canoes and Different Drummers." *Wisconsin Trails* (Summer, 1979), Vol. 20, No. 2.

DENSMORE, FRANCES. "Chippewa Customs." *Bulletin of the Bureau of American Ethnology* No. 86. Washington: Bureau of American Ethnology, 1929.

FLINT INSTITUTE OF ARTS. *The Art of the Great Lakes Indians*. Flint, Michigan: Flint Institute of Arts, 1973.

GUY, CAMIL. *Le Canot d'écorce à Weymontaching.* Musée national de l'homme. Montréal: Éditions de l'Aurore, 1977.

HYDE, GEORGE E. *Indians of the Woodlands.* Norman, Oklahoma: University of Oklahoma Press, 1962.

JENNESS, DIAMOND. *Indians of Canada.* National Museum of Canada, Bulletin No. 65, Ottawa: 1955.

LEMOINE, GEORGES. *Dictionnaire Français-Algonquin.* Chicoutimi, Quebec: G. Delisle, 1909.

LORTIE, GÉRARD. *La raquette.* Montréal: Éditions du Jour, 1972.

MATHEVET, J. C. *Ka Titc Jezos* (Life of Christ). Amos, Québec: Les Missionnaires Oblats de Marie Immaculée, 1968.

McPHEE, JOHN. *The Survival of the Bark Canoe.* New York: Farrar, Straus and Giroux, 1975.

ORCHARD, WILLIAM. "The Technique of Porcupine Quill Decoration Among the North American Indians." (Vol. 4, No. 1.) New York: Museum of the American Indian, Heye Foundation, 1916.

QUIMBY, GEORGE I. *Indian Life in the Upper Great Lakes.* Chicago: University of Chicago Press, 1960.

RITZENTHALER, ROBERT E. "The Building of a Chippewa Indian Birchbark Canoe." *Bulletin of the Public Museum of the City of Milwaukee* (November, 1950), Vol. 19, No. 2, pp. 53-90.

RITZENTHALER, ROBERT E. *The Woodland Indians of the Western Great Lakes.* Garden City, New York: The Natural History Press, 1970.

RIVER DESERT ALGONQUIN BAND. *Tales from the River Desert.* Maniwaki, Quebec: River Desert Band, 1976.

SCHNEIDER, RICHARD C. *Crafts of the North American Indians.* New York: Van Nostrand Reinhold, 1972.

SIMARD, CYRIL. *Artisanat québécois: Indiens et Esquimaux.* Montréal: Éditions de l'Homme, 1977.

SNELL, GEORGE F., Jr. "Pine Country Hiawatha." *Sports Afield* (August, 1945), Vol. 120, No. 2.

SPECK, FRANK G. *Family Hunting Territories and Social Life of Various Algonkian Bands of the Ottawa Valley.* (Memoir 70, Canada Department of Mines Geological Survey, No. 8, Anthropological Series.) Ottawa: Government Printing Bureau, 1915.

SPECK, FRANK G. "River Desert Algonquins of Quebec." *Indian Notes.* (Vol. 4, No. 1) New York: Museum of the American Indian, Heye Foundation, 1927.

THAVENET, ABBÉ. *Dictionnaire Algonquin-Français.* Oka, Quebec: manuscript, 1815?

VASTOKAS, JOAN M., and VASTOKAS, ROMAS K. *Sacred Art of the Algonkians.* Peterborough, Ontario: Mansard Press, 1973.

YARNELL, JEAN. *Algonquin Ethnobotany: An Interpretation of Aboriginal Adaptation in Southwestern Quebec.* Ann Arbor, Michigan: University of Michigan (unpublished paper), 1973.

Index

(numbers in italics refer to illustration)

oo